YOUR
FAMILY TREE
ONLINE

Visit our How To website at **www.howto.co.uk**

At **www.howto.co.uk** you can engage in conversation with our authors – all of whom have 'been there and done that' in their specialist fields. You can get access to special offers and additional content but most importantly you will be able to engage with, and become a part of, a wide and growing community of people just like yourself.

At **www.howto.co.uk** you'll be able to talk and share tips with people who have similar interests and are facing similar challenges in their lives. People who, just like you, have the desire to change their lives for the better – be it through moving to a new country, starting a new business, growing their own vegetables, or writing a novel.

At **www.howto.co.uk** you'll find the support and encouragement you need to help make your aspirations a reality.

You can go direct to **www.your-family-tree-online.co.uk** which is part of the main How To site.

How To Books strives to present authentic, inspiring, practical information in their books. Now, when you buy a title from **How To Books,** you get even more than just words on a page.

YOUR FAMILY TREE ONLINE

How to trace your ancestry from your own computer

Graeme Davis

howtobooks

Published by How To Books Ltd,
Spring Hill House, Spring Hill Road,
Begbroke, Oxford OX5 1RX
Tel: (01865) 375794. Fax: (01865) 379162
info@howtobooks.co.uk
www.howtobooks.co.uk

How To Books greatly reduce the carbon footprint of their books by sourcing their
typesetting and printing in the UK.

British Library Cataloguing in Publication Data
A catalogue record for this book is available from the British Library

ISBN: 978 1 84528 344 5

Produced for How To Books by Deer Park Productions, Tavistock, Devon
Typeset by PDQ Typesetting, Newcastle-under-Lyme, Staffs.
Printed and bound by Cromwell Press Group, Trowbridge, Wiltshire

NOTE: The material contained in this book is set out in good faith for general guidance
and no liability can be accepted for loss or expense incurred as a result of relying in
particular circumstances on statements made in the book. Laws and regulations are
complex and liable to change, and readers should check the current position with the
relevant authorities before making personal arrangements.

Contents

Welcome!   **1**
What you can achieve   1
Who is this book for?   3
What you can expect   4
How long will it take?   4
Activity – Getting started   4

1   What the Internet Offers the Genealogist   **9**
Vaue of the Internet   9
Activity – Have you Googled?   12

2   How to Start   **14**
First Principles   14
Activity – Do these first   15
Activity – What do you know about your family?   15
Activity – For each relative   17

3   Finding Records of Birth, Marriage and Death   **18**
Sources for births, marriages and deaths   18
National and state registration offices   22
Activity – Find your country's BMD   23
Using national BMD records   24
Activity – Find your ancestors in BMD records   25
The International Genealogical Index   27
Activity – Discover the most important single website   30
Activity – Working with the IGI advanced search   31

4   Using Census Records   **33**
What are census records?   33
Activity – Locate census records   35
Years censuses are available for   36
Information on censuses   37
Accuracy of censuses   37
The 1911 census   38
The 1881 census   40
Activity – Searching the census   40

5   Other Major Sources   **42**
Cyndi's List   42
Activity – Countries on Cyndi's List   43
Activity – Cyndi and solutions for problems   45
Religious collections   45
Activity – Nonconformist ancestors   46
Regional collections   46
Activity – Find local record offices   46
Look-up exchanges   47
Activity – Ask someone!   47
Finding relatives   48
Activity – Getting in touch   48
Pay sites   49
Activity – Pay sites   49

6   Military   **50**
Military records   50
Activity – Commonwealth War Graves Commission   52
Activity – Regimental histories   52
Activity – Battle of the Somme   54

7   Wills and Where to Find them Online   **55**
The problem with wills   55
Activity – Thinking about wills   55

8   Migration   **56**
Immigration and emigration   56
Activity – Passenger arrival lists   57

9   Newspapers   **58**
What newspapers offer   58
Activity – Connecting through local newspapers   59
An example of a family story in a newspaper article   60

10   Occupations   **61**
Job titles   61
Activity – Understand your ancestor's job   62

11   The Poor and Workhouse Records   **63**
Records of the poor   63
Activity – Understanding nineteenth century poverty   63

12 Noble Ancestors   **65**
Finding noble ancestors   65
Titles and coats of arms   67
A warning!   67
Activity – Heraldry and genealogy   69
A note on titles   69

13 Directories   **71**
Working with directories   71
Activity – Directories   73

14 School and University Records   **75**
Schools   75
Activity – Schools   76
Universities   77
Activity – Finding ancestors at university   78

15 Working with the Wider Context   **79**
Local history   79
Activity – Accessing local history sources   80
Maps   80
General history   82
Activity – Finding context   82
Activity – Finding maps   83
Activity – View a timeline   83

16 Family Medical History   **84**
Activity – Focusing on close relatives   84
Activity – Identifying sources of medical information   85
Twins   86
Life expectancy   87

17 DNA   **89**
DNA and inherited disease   89
DNA and family medical history   89
The new frontier   90
Deep DNA   91
Ethnic DNA   92
Surname studies   94
Warning!   96
Activity – Testing services   96
DNA studies   96

18 Working with Names   99
Sources of British surnames   99
History of surnames   100
Changing your surname   102
Surname profiling   103
Activity – Estimating kinship   105
Clans   105
First names   106
Activity – Working with surnames   107
Activity – Do you belong to a clan?   108
Activity – Working with first names   108

19 Recording Your Family Tree   109
Charts   109
Books   110
Activity – Charts   111
Activity – Books   111
Activity – Posting your family tree to the World Wide Web   112
What you can expect   112
How long will it take?   113

20 Online Recording Options   114
Activity – Data control   114
Option 1 – Ancestry.com   115
Activity 1 – Know your goals   118
Activity 2 – Share your family tree   118
Option 2 – GenesReunited.com   119
Option 3 – Your own website   120
More about Ancestry.com   120
More about GenesReunited.com   123
Other companies   124
Avoiding re-entry of data   126
More about your own website   127
Activity 3 – View examples   129

21 Problems of Online Trees   131
Online family trees and drawing family trees   131
GEDCOM problems   131
Libel   133
Confidential information   133

22 Finding Living Relatives   134
Contacting lost relatives   134
Site-moderated emails   135
Personal emails   135
Meeting relatives   136

23 Genealogical Miscellany   137
Photographs   137
Activity – Photographs   144
Family stories and oral history   144
Activity – Be willing to believe stories   145
Sharing research costs   145
Newspaper cuttings   146
Activity – *The Times*   147
Publications   147
Activity – Find an ancestor's book   148
Personal belongings and jewellery   148
Activity – Looking at personal possessions   149
Hair samples   149

24 Accent and Dialect   151
Activity – Collecting information   151
Activity – What does it mean?   152

25 Final   153

Key Websites   154
Name sites   154
Sources for births, marriages and deaths   154
Census sites   154
Pedigree sites   155
National variants of Ancestry.com   155
Heraldry   155
Extensive list of genealogy links   156
Look-ups   156
Directories   156
Charts   156
Some other great sites   156

Index   158

Welcome!

Welcome to the world of genealogy and the internet! Using this *How To* Guide you can find your way through the mass of online sources to discover more about your family history. You can see how your ancestors lived and how they fitted in with their age, you can draw up a family tree – in short you can become a genealogist.

Everyone has their own reason for starting. Maybe Great Aunt Maud has sent that long-promised letter with her recollections of family stories dating back well over a century. In it are names and descriptions of events that perhaps you didn't know about, or maybe your memory is jogged and you remember people that you heard someone speak about many years ago and had all but forgotten. Maybe there's a browning photograph showing the face of an ancestor. Or an old postcard someone wrote, or the book-plate of a school-prize Bible.

Yet however much Great Aunt Maud has sent, or however great your existing family tree knowledge might be, it is never quite enough, and you will want to find out more. This book sets out what you can do to trace your family tree using the internet.

WHAT YOU CAN ACHIEVE

With this *How To* book, *Your Family Tree OnLine*, you will be able to make progress researching a genealogy. In this guide there is everything you need to take a family line back many hundreds of years.

You can think of family tree resources in terms of three great collections: those from the age of Queen Victoria, those subsequent, and those earlier. There is a fourth area for the late mediaeval records, and while with luck and persistence you might end up using these, to be honest you will be lucky to find a line that goes back this far.

- In Britain, the golden age for the genealogist is the Victorian Age (1837–1901). Victoria's reign started in the same year as the introduction of national birth, marriage and death registration in England and Wales, and ended with a key UK census. Seven census returns fall in the years of Victoria's reign. This is the period where the most progress can be made.

- There are plenty of records subsequent to Queen Victoria's reign, including the magnificent 1911 census, though many of these later records are subject to restrictions of access in order to protect people who may be living today. There are more likely to be costs accessing them. Nonetheless, progress can be made in tracing a family in the twentieth century.

- Prior to Queen Victoria's reign the records are more challenging to search. They may perhaps be more rewarding also. In the British Isles lines can readily be traced in the eighteenth century, and with increasing difficulty through the seventeenth and even sixteenth centuries.

- In the late Middle Ages only noble families left enough records to be traced. In the early Middle Ages just about the only lines that can be traced are the royal lines and a handful of noble families. Further back no European family bridges the gap of the Dark Ages and therefore no one of European ancestry can today trace a family line back to the Classical World.

You can reasonably expect to trace a family line through the twentieth and nineteenth centuries and into the eighteenth century, and with tenacity have a good chance of making more progress. If you have luck and put in the effort, there are lines that do indeed trace even as far as the end of the Middle Ages. The very newest approach is though the rise of DNA analysis, which offers some possibilities for 'deep' genealogy, genealogy going back thousands of years. Using DNA resources you may be able to identify an ancestor from hundreds or in theory even thousands of years ago.

WHO IS THIS BOOK FOR?

This *How To* guide is for anyone who wants to research a family. Using the resources here you can advance your family tree without travelling to national and regional record offices. Wherever you live and wherever your family lived, you can make progress with researching your family. The emphasis for this guide is on the British Isles and those English-speaking countries where ancestry goes back to Britain. There's a lot in this book however that is relevant to any country in the world.

This book does not assume any prior knowledge of how to trace your family tree. Notwithstanding, it does have material likely to be of interest even to experienced genealogists. The online tools are the new frontier of genealogy, and even the experienced genealogist should find something new described here.

What you can expect

You will know more about your family by the time you have
finished this guide than you do now. Just how much progress you
make depends in part on luck – where your ancestors came from,
how common or unusual their surname is, just what records have
been preserved and made available through the internet – and
how much time and energy you put into it. Families can be traced,
though there are often blocks, where missing records provide
challenges. Often there are 'work-arounds' where the problems of
missing records can be minimised, so a block should usually be
regarded as a temporary problem. Blocks and 'work-arounds' do
however take time.

How long will it take?

You can make some progress in a very few hours. Or you can
spend a lifetime researching a genealogy. Ten hours of work
should be enough to yield some interesting results.

ACTIVITY

Getting started
Here's something for everyone – and it's quick and easy.

▶ Go to: http://www.nationaltrustnames.org.uk

▶ Type in your surname, or a surname you are interested in.

▶ Select the year 1881.

▶ See the distribution of this surname in England, Wales and
Scotland (unfortunately Ireland is not yet included).

▶

Least   **Most**

Fig. 1. The surname Curthoys on National Trust Names, an example of a
surname with a very strong localisation.

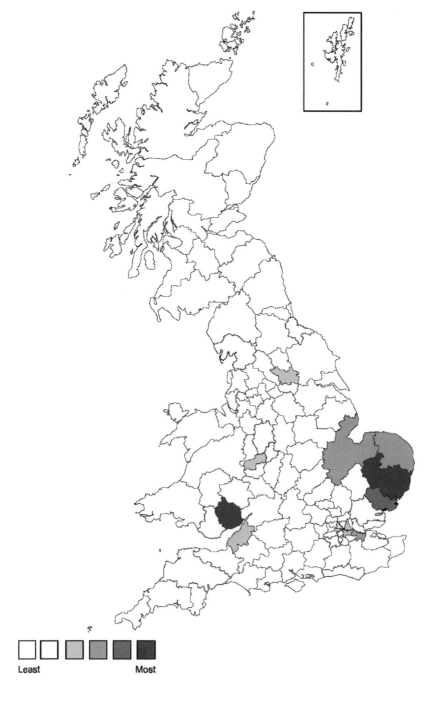

Fig. 2. The surname Everson on National Trust Names – an example of a surname with several distinct localisations.

The maps (see Figures 1 and 2) you retrieve need some interpretation:

▶ Is there one centre for the surname? This is the place of origin of the surname. There is a high degree of probability that all people who bear this surname are related.

▶ Are there two or three centres? Probably this indicates an early branching of the family, with several branches becoming established.

▶ Is the surname widely spread, found in most parts of Britain? This probably indicates polygenesis, where the surname has evolved separately many times and bearers of the surname are not therefore related.

Examples of monogenesis (a single founder for the surname) include many surnames that we all recognise as unusual. For example, 'Curnow' appears only in the toe of Cornwall, the area around Penzance. Almost certainly there was just one Curnow who founded the line, and probably he lived as recently as the late eighteenth century. Similarly, 'Curthoys' appears in South Gloucestershire and North Somersetshire (around the city of Bristol), with an outlier in Wolverhampton. This name is slightly more common than Curnow, and the first 'Curthoys' is probably late seventeenth century.

Names such as 'Everson', 'Norton', 'Palmer' and 'Bates' are likely to be monogenetic, but with a much earlier first ancestor. By the time of the 1881 census, these names are widely distributed, though not across the whole country.

Many names are polygenetic, with many points of origin. My own surname 'Davis' is an example. It is often Welsh, but it can also be English, Scottish, Irish or Jewish. There was no single first Davis, but rather many. Similarly, such names as 'Smith', 'Jones',

'Martin', 'Hall', 'Clift' and many, many more have many different individuals who were first bearers.

If the surname you are interested in is monogenetic, you have an idea of the place of origin of your ancestors. Even if it is polygenetic you may get an idea of where it is from. For example, 'Martin' is far more common in the West Country than elsewhere in the British Isles.

1

What the Internet Offers the Genealogist

VALUE OF THE INTERNET

In a nutshell the internet is the most exciting and most powerful single tool available to the genealogist.

When records first came available through the internet many professionals were dismissive. They thought the internet was never going to compete with the traditional archives, and that the idea of tracing a family tree online would never be possible. How wrong they were! Today it is unthinkable to trace a family without using the internet, and every single area of family tree research is to some extent covered by the internet. Once the internet supplemented archives; now it is the other way round, with archives supplementing the internet sources.

A key concept is that you should regard the internet as an enormous index, which directs you to resources. Often the records themselves are online; alternatively you may need to send off for them. Sometimes transcriptions of records are available online, which are as accurate as the person who entered the information. In such cases you really should check back to the originals.

The sorts of materials that are available online are as follows:

■ Very many family trees are available on the internet. It is possible to link in to an existing tree and make fast progress in this way.

■ Very many researchers have posted their details, so that it is possible to contact fellow researchers, who are likely to be your distant relatives.

■ The internet offers access to documents, either transcribed or as pdf images of the original documents – or both.

■ The internet offers access to indexes of documents. Access to the documents themselves can then be organised.

Of course the internet cannot offer everything. The biggest area not covered by the internet is the importance of speaking with relatives. Most family trees start with the memories and recollections of relatives. All family trees benefit from some help from traditional, non-internet sources somewhere along the line. However, the internet has become the single most powerful tool for research, and even a tool which can be used without reference to relatives or archives.

Provision of online materials is excellent for the UK. This book concentrates on these UK records, though it does not ignore non-UK sources. Additionally, many of the concepts set out here are applicable to researching families worldwide. In general, online records for Europe and North America are good, as are those for Australia and New Zealand. Elsewhere coverage is patchy, both in terms of records that have been preserved and in terms of what is available on the internet. Yet even in the case of countries with poor provision of records usually something can be done. At the very least the advent of genetic tools in genealogy research means

Google "aquila bates   Search   Advanced Sear
                                                    Preferences
                                           Personalized based on your web histo

Web Books   Results 1 - 8 of 8 for "aquila bates. (0.5

RootsWeb's WorldConnect Project: Bates Family Lineage ENG/Cape ...
Aquila BATES was born 18 JUN 1765, was christened 4 JUL 1765 in Newenden, ... **Aquila
BATES** (John BATES4, John BATES3, Samuel BATES2, Thomas BATES1) was born ...
wc.rootsweb.ancestry.com/cgi-bin/igm.cgi?op=REG&db=mbates&id=I617 - Similar pages -

Old Romney Tithe award schedule 112KB
0. 1. 6 0. 1. 2 0.13. 1. Frances Anne Kenrick Sheet 4. Stephen Kirkbank Magdalen College,
Oxford, **Aquila Bates** Lawrence Reeve John Longley Ralph Collyer, 22 ...
www.kentarchaeology.org.uk/Research/Maps/OLD/02.htm - 112k -
Cached - Similar pages -

Aquila Bates City, MO - Web Search - Switchboard.com
Aquila Bates City, MO on Switchboard.com, featuring **Aquila Bates** City, MO in web web
search.
www.switchboard.com/webresults.htm?qcat=web&qkw=Aquila+Bates%20City,%20MO - 66k -
Cached - Similar pages -

John Bates - Records - Ancestry.com
Spouse & Children. Mary Johnson. Unknown-Unknown. Barbara Bates; Samuel Bates; **Aquila
Bates**. Additional Resources. Search Census & voter Lists ...
records.ancestry.com/John_Bates_1731_records.ashx?pid=99661290&gss=seo - 30k -
Cached - Similar pages -

Parliamentary Papers - Google Books Result
by Great Britain Parliament. House of Commons ... - 1834 - Great Britain
CORPORATION OF NEW ROMNEY. CHARITABLE FUNDS. Thomas Baker, of New Romney,
gentleman, by will dated 8th July 1728, gave unto the mayor, jurats and commonalty ...
books.google.com/books?id=3EcSAAAAYAAJ...

Members researching George A Bates - Ancestry.com
Name: George **Aquila Bates**. Birth: 31 Mar 1867 - Elham, Kent. Death: 29 Mar 1941 -
Edmonton, Middlesex. Residence: 1881 - Tottenham, Middlesex, England ...
www.ancestry.com/community/researchers.aspx?fn=George%20A&ln=Bates - 60k -
Cached - Similar pages -

John Bates - OneWorldTree - Ancestry.co.uk
Birth: dd mm 1764 - city, Wor, England Marriage: date - city, On Severn, England. **Aquila
Bates** Spouse: name surname. F: John Bates. M: Mary Johnson ...
search.ancestry.com/cgi-bin/sse.dll?_8000C002=Barnabas&_8000C003=Bates... - 122k -
Cached - Similar pages -

Fig. 3. A Google search result on an unusual name – Aquila Bates.

that something can be discovered about the ancestry of every human being.

Have you Googled?
The most basic way of searching for your ancestors on the web is to use Google or another internet search engine. In the region of one-fifth of British people born in the nineteenth century or before are mentioned in an internet source which can be found simply through using Google. The key to finding them is the format of your search.

For names which are not too common – something like 'Henry Brooks Bates' (or 'Aquila Bates', see Figure 3) – you can try the following:

▶ Simply enter the name in the Google search box.

▶ Better enter the name in speech marks so that Google searches for the exact phrase. A feature of Google is that you need only the opening speech marks, so 'Henry Brooks Bates.

▶ Enter the name as surname first: 'Bates Henry Brooks'.

▶ Try with a middle initial only: 'Henry B Bates' and 'Bates Henry B'.

▶ Try without the middle name 'Henry Bates' and 'Bates Henry'.

▶ For women, try both maiden and married surname.

Further search terms can be entered in addition to the name in all these formats. If you are looking for a common name, then a further search term is likely to be essential. You can try a place associated with the ancestor. This might be a village, a town, a county. A search for 'Daniel Clift' is frustrating because it generates too many possibilities, but 'Daniel Clift' and 'Bramley' (a village in Hampshire) found together may well be useful. You can try an occupation. 'Walter Harris' is not useful, but 'Walter Harris' and 'stone-mason' looks more promising. With a married couple, you can try to trace the names of both together. It is also worth trying a search for the name of your ancestor plus the year of birth, as many genealogists reference ancestors in this way.

Google searches in these multiple formats do take a few minutes, but they do often yield results. Looking at the results and checking that they really do relate to your ancestors can take some time also. If you try googling in these multiple formats the names of a dozen ancestors born in the nineteenth century or before, you would be unlucky not to get a hit or two which is relevant.

2

How to Start

FIRST PRINCIPLES

So you are ready to start. These first principles should help with all genealogical research:

1. Always move from the known to the unknown. What doesn't work is to start with a famous person in the past, or a family legend, and try to find a line forward in time to you. Always start with yourself, move back through the ancestors you know, and gradually build up information about earlier generations.

2. Internet genealogy is now the most powerful single source for researching a family tree, and the fastest-growing source of genealogical information. Much can be done to research your family using the internet alone. But results will be better if other sources are also used. It is important therefore to regard the internet as one tool among many. Today the sort of tools available to the genealogist are:

    (a) Your family: what relatives can tell you about your family, and what photographs and written records may be preserved within your family.

    (b) Archival records. These are the paper-based and micro-fiche-based records available worldwide both in national repositories and local record offices.

(c) Records of social, cultural and local history which can contextualise information about your family.

(d) DNA testing.

(e) The internet.

Today the internet is the one tool that is indispensable to the genealogist. It is now unthinkable to research any family tree without using it. It is possible to make progress without some or even all of the other tools.

ACTIVITY

Do these first

This is a difficult thing to say in a *How To* guide called *Your Family Tree Online*, but here goes: your very first steps are best taken off-line!

The activities needed to get started are as follows:

What do you know about your family?

Sit down with a (large) piece of paper and write out a family tree of names and relationships as far as you know them.

Where possible add concrete detail: date and place of birth, marriage and death, occupation.

Where you are unsure of your facts, estimate dates or put forward probable places – but make sure you show clearly that these are estimates or best guesses.

Ask relatives. In particular get in touch with relatives you rarely see or speak to. Ring, write, email, visit.

Family research is a great reason for getting in touch with relatives. Remember that relatives by marriage may also know a lot about your family.

Right from the outset you need to be aware of some rule of thumb conventions for estimating dates:

▶ The genealogical convention is that the average length of a generation is 30 years. If you know the date of birth of a child, assume that the parents were born 30 years previously. If you know dates of birth of two or more brothers and sisters, you can produce a date range for the parents' birth 30 years back from that of two or more children.

▶ Genealogists assume three generations per century – which it has to be said doesn't quite tally with the convention of a generation being 30 years. Chances are your great-grandparents were born about a hundred years before you.

▶ Genealogists assume men are aged 25 at marriage, women aged 20. In fact these ages change a lot from community to community, and a better guide is often to look at ages at marriage you actually know in the immediate family, and make your assumption based on that.

▶ Using the assumptions set out here you can estimate a date of birth from the birth date of children or the date of marriage. You should think of it as plus or minus ten years, which is broad enough to catch most possibilities but still narrow enough to search most online records.

▶ You can use these assumptions to go back two or even three generations. Two generations back you will probably find that the range is still just plus or minus ten years, as on average variances tend to balance one another out. Even three generations back plus or minus ten to 15 years is probably reasonable, and still searchable.

▶ Dates of death are hardest to estimate. You can often work out a year when you are sure someone must have been alive and a year by when you are sure they are dead. If the range is 20 years or less, express it as the middle year plus or minus ten years (or less if you can manage). If there is more than a 20-year date range, you really have to accept that you just don't know.

▶ Ancestors who lived to a great age tend to be remembered, often with considerable exaggeration. Someone who was 'nearly a hundred' at death may well turn out to be quite a few years younger.

ACTIVITY

For each relative

Answer as many of these questions as possible, as fully as possible, for every relative. Include spouses, as information about spouses can often help to trace your relative.

▶ What was their full name?

▶ When were they born? Who were they older or younger than?

▶ Where were they born? Where did they grow up? Where did they go to school?

▶ Who did they marry, when and where? Who were their children?

▶ What was their job? Were they in the armed forces?

▶ When and where did they die?

You will quickly discover that relatives are rarely good sources of precise information. Indeed asking a list of questions such as those above may even cause embarrassment as most people simply won't know. Every area is problematic. For example, people are often known by nicknames which may or may not resolve into their real name, ages are slippery, place of birth frequently not known, and details of deaths comfortably forgotten. A particular problem is nicknames. Jack may be Jack, or may be John. Bert may be Robert, or could be Herbert or Hubert or Cuthbert. First names and middle names are often swapped round, and many go through life known only by their middle name. Dates are usually problematic. Places of birth are rarely specifically remembered – you are more likely to find that someone remembers where an ancestor grew up rather than where they were born. Additionally, family stories often muddle generations. Listen to what you are told, and take it all with a grain of salt.

3

Finding Records of Birth, Marriage and Death

SOURCES FOR BIRTHS, MARRIAGES AND DEATHS

The key records which stitch together a family tree are those of birth, marriage and death. Within the British Isles there is generally more than one source for each. Records of birth can be found as:

■ Birth certificates, the national records. The law requires that the date of every child's birth is registered.

■ Records of christening in parish registers. Traditionally christenings have taken place shortly after birth, and often the birth date is also recorded.

■ Newspaper announcements of birth are relatively rare before the late twentieth century, but they do exist.

■ Family records, for example in family bibles.

Records of marriage can be found as:

■ Marriage certificates, the national records. The law requires that all marriages are registered.

- Records of marriages in parish registers, or the registers of other places of worship.

- Records of the banns of a marriage, or of the licence obtained.

- Newspaper announcements of engagements and marriages are reasonably common from the late nineteenth century.

Records of deaths can be found as:

- Death certificates, the national records. The law requires that all deaths are registered.

- Records of burials in parish registers.

- Memorial inscriptions, including grave stones in a cemetery, memorials within a church, war memorials, memorials at crematoria.

- Newspaper announcements of deaths, and sometimes newspaper obituaries. These are reasonably common from the late nineteenth century.

- Mourning cards may be preserved by families.

- Children's deaths may be recorded in a family bible.

The collection and preservation of all this birth, marriage and death data is excellent in the British Isles. Access is relatively straightforward.

Birth certificates

Birth certificates exist for almost all births. Inevitably, there have been a small number that have not been registered, but the need later in life for a birth certificate has tended to ensure that even those initially excluded are later added. Birth certificates in Britain are public documents, which means that anyone can obtain anyone's birth certificate. If you want to see the Queen's birth certificate, or the Prime Minister's, or absolutely anyone's, you can get it. Anyone can have a look at your birth certificate. This is a remarkable position, as many countries (including the USA) do place restrictions on access to these vital records. For example, if you want to see the birth certificate from Hawaii of US President Obama, you won't be able to. Parish registers of christenings are similarly available in Britain without restriction on access. Often two copies exist – the original parish record, and a copy sent to the bishop (called Bishop's Transcripts). Preservation of British Isles parish registers has been excellent, though there are gaps. Adult baptisms are similarly well preserved.

Marriage certificates

Marriage certificates and parish register records of marriage exist whenever a formal marriage took place. In past ages, most couples did formally register their marriage, though there are of course exceptions. Particularly in cities, it was possible for Victorian couples to live together without the formality of a marriage. Bear in mind that the bride's name will be recorded as her name at the time of marriage, which if she is a widow will not be her maiden name. Divorce records do exist, effectively from the early twentieth century, but are unlikely to play a big part in the research of most genealogists. Rather couples separated, and may sometimes have remarried without benefit of a divorce.

Death certificates

Death certificates and records of burial (and more recently of cremation) are a near-comprehensive set of records. There has long been a bureaucratic system around death and funeral arrangements which has left a paper trail. The one drawback for the genealogist is that the provision of indexes for these records online is not as good as for birth and marriage records.

Problems locating certificates

If you can't find a birth certificate, it is just about possible that the birth was not registered (though this is most unlikely). If you can't find a marriage certificate then probably the marriage did not take place. But if you cannot find a death certificate then almost certainly you are doing something wrong. Every genealogist will have a death they just can't find, leading to jokes to the effect that the ancestor must have been buried in the cabbage patch. Yet realistically it has to be the genealogist that is wrong. Bear in mind that a woman might marry and so change her name – the single most common reason for being unable to find a woman's death. Registration is as accurate as the informant. Names may be garbled, ages may be wrong.

Use of certificates

These records of birth, marriage and death are the framework of a family tree. Records of birth and christening usually give information about the child's parents, taking lines back a generation. Records of marriage typically give information about the fathers of both bride and groom. Death records are the least useful for genealogists as they tend to give relatively little information about the person's family. Memorial inscriptions tend to point forward (giving the names of the children of the deceased) rather than back.

NATIONAL AND STATE REGISTRATION OFFICES

Most countries or states have national repositories for records of births, marriages and deaths, and many have had for 150 years or more (a major exception is the US, where these records go back just a hundred years). Often birth, marriage and death (BMD) records are called *vital* records. In some jurisdictions (notably the US) divorce records are treated as a fourth category of vital records.

Information given on certificates of birth, marriage and death is remarkably consistent from country to country.

On a birth certificate you can expect to find the full name, date and place of birth, names of both parents, usually including the mother's maiden name, and occupation of both parents – though frequently the space for the mother's occupation is left blank. A few countries record information about the parents' marriage. Usually the name of the person who records the birth is given, very often one of the parents. Birth certificates provide solid information for taking a family tree back another generation.

Marriage certificates usually give the full name and occupation of the bride and groom, the age of both, and the date and place of marriage. Most record some information about the families of each, typically the names and occupations of the two fathers. The place of marriage is likely to be set out precisely – a particular church perhaps, or synagogue or other place of worship, or perhaps a town hall. Frequently, there is information about the religious framework of a ceremony – it might be according to the rites of a specific Christian church. Names of witnesses are usually given, and as these are often family members they can be clues to other people in the family. Marriage certificates are one of the most useful documents for genealogists.

Death certificates usually give full name, age at death, place of death and cause of death. Usually the name of the person who registered the death is given, and very often this person is a relative. Sometimes information is recorded about the date and place of birth. For the purposes of building a family tree, death certificates are the least useful as they tend to point forward rather than back (perhaps forward to a child who registers the death of a parent), and give little guidance on family relationships. They are also prone to error. In particular, beware ages and dates of birth which are frequently wrong. Cause of death can sometimes be frustrating – I have even seen 'old age' given as the cause of death.

ACTIVITY

Find your country's BMD

For England and Wales, national records have been kept since 1837, and you can access the indexes online. Scotland and Ireland (both Northern Ireland and the Irish Republic) have their own systems. The Channel Islands and Isle of Man do things differently again. To start look at the following key sites:

▶ http://www.bmdindex.co.uk/ Birth, Marriage and Death Certificates – BMD Index 1837–2004 – great source, but there is a charge.

▶ http://www.freebmd.org.uk/ FreeBMD (see Figure 4) is an ongoing project – at the moment, its coverage is excellent prior to 1914, but patchy subsequently. More records are being added, so the position is improving.

For the US, each state has its own system, and it is complicated. Fortunately, there is a website which guides you through the maze:

▶ http://www.vitalrec.com This website provides information on how to obtain vital records from each state and territory of the US.

Similarly, Canada and Australia have state-based systems, and specialist websites to help navigation:

▶ Canada: http://globalgenealogy.com/globalgazette

▶ Australia: http://www.coraweb.com.au/bdmaut.htm

Ireland has its own special issues. The key website is the Irish Family History Resource: http://www.eneclann.ie

For other countries, see Cyndi's List (Chapter 5, below).

USING NATIONAL BMD RECORDS

National records of births, marriages and deaths are comprehensive collections which aim to record everyone without exception. For this reason these records are the building blocks of genealogical research. The quality of the records is very high. Gaps are very rare, and you should expect full coverage for your ancestors. If you can't find a record, assume you are searching wrongly. Maybe the event took place outside of the nation whose records you are searching. Maybe you are some years out with the dates and need to search further. Maybe you have the name wrong – perhaps your ancestor disliked a first name used at birth and instead went through life using a middle name, or even adopted an entirely different name. Women change their name through marriage – remember that a woman who marries for a second time is recorded at the time of that marriage with the surname of her first husband, not her maiden name, and similarly remember that a woman who remarries late in life will die with her last husband's surname.

Unfortunately, in most countries these records are not available on the web. This will change, but the process is slow. However, the indexes to these records often are available, and this is a major service to the internet genealogist. Pre-internet it was necessary to go to a national record office, usually in the capital city, search through paper-based indexes – a very slow task – then request a certificate, which could take anything from days to many weeks to be produced. Now it is usually far quicker and more convenient to search the indexes on the web than through the paper or microfiche index at a national record office. Once you have the index record of your ancestor's birth, marriage or death you can send off for a certificate of the birth, marriage or death from the national record office. There will be a charge, set by the appropriate government office. In Britain, these charges are modest (around £7), though the dedicated genealogist can wish to see a considerable number.

ACTIVITY

Find your ancestors in BMD records

BIRTHS
- ▶ You need your ancestor's full name.
- ▶ You need a date of birth, or at least a good estimate.
- ▶ You need at least the country or state of birth and if possible a precise location.
- ▶ You may need other information to confirm that you have found the right person, for example the name of the father. Usually you have to buy the certificate to check this information.

MARRIAGES
- ▶ In theory, all you need are the surnames of bride and groom. The bride's surname at marriage is usually essential.

 **Search**

To search FreeBMD enter the details of the search below. A fuller explanation of how to get the most out of your search is <u>here</u>.To select and deselect multiple choices hold down CTRL as you click the mouse. The earliest possible date is 1837.

Type	All Types Births Deaths Marriages	Districts	All Districts Aberayron (to Jun1936) Aberconwy (from Sep1975) Abergavenny (to 1958) Aberystwyth (to Jun1936) Abingdon Acle (1939-Mar1974) Alcester Alderbury (to Jun1895) Aldershot (Dec1932-Mar1974) Aldridge & Brownhills (Jun1966-Mar1974) Aled (Dec1935-Mar1974) Alnwick (to 1936) Alresford (to Sep1932)

Surname

First name(s)

Spouse/Mother surname

Spouse first name(s)

Death age/DoB

Date range   Mar ☐   to   Dec ☐

Volume/Page   /   Counties

Options
☐ Mono
☐ Exact match on first names
☐ Phonetic search surnames
☐ Match only recorded ages

Counties		
All Counties Anglesey (to Mar1974) Avon (from Jun1974) Bedfordshire Berkshire Breconshire (to Mar1974)		

[Find] [Count] [Reset]

<u>Advanced Facilities</u>

<u>FreeBMD Main Page</u>

Saved search

Filename:

[Browse...]

[Find Additional] [View Saved]   Help

Fig. 4. The Free BMD search entry screen.

▶ In practice first names help, and if the surnames are common may be essential.

▶ You can find a marriage even if you are unsure of the date. It is practical to search a large number of years as the check provided by two names ensures you have the right marriage.

▶ You have to be searching in the right country or state, but aside from this you need very little information about the place of marriage.

DEATHS

▶ You need your ancestor's full name.

▶ You need at least an approximate year of death.

▶ You need information about age, and place of death.

▶ Death records are the hardest to find, and give the least information when found.

THE INTERNATIONAL GENEALOGICAL INDEX

Prior to general registration of births, marriages and deaths – and often recorded in parallel with these national records up to today – are religious records. Within the Christian tradition these are predominantly records of christenings, marriages and burials. Other faiths may record other life events which are seen as important.

Once these records were housed where they had been created, and access was by an appointment with a parish priest or minister. Increasingly, they have found their way into local record offices, though still access is by a personal visit and potentially lengthy search, or by using the expensive services of a private researcher.

Amazingly, the internet has provided a solution. By far the biggest collection of birth, marriage and death records – online or offline – is

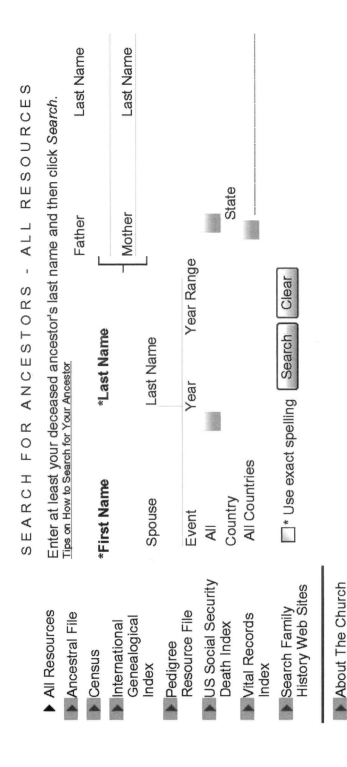

Fig. 5. Family Search advanced search page.
FamilySearch.org is an official website of The Church of Jesus Christ of Latter-day Saints © 2008.

provided free by the Jesus Christ Church of Latter Day Saints, commonly known as the Mormons, and called the International Genealogical Index (IGI). The Mormons believe that the Gospel is taught both in this life and also in the next, and that those who did not learn it while alive can learn it after their death. However, there is a Mormon religious belief which requires Mormon baptism as well as acceptance of the Gospel in order to go to heaven. Mormons believe the only way the dead can be baptised is if a relative who is a Mormon baptises them posthumously. This religious belief has led to a moral requirement for Mormons to trace their ancestors, and the creation by the Mormons of a massive genealogical resource which has as its primary purpose that of enabling Mormons to trace their ancestors in order to baptise them posthumously.

The Mormon records aim ultimately to cover absolutely every country and age, and at the moment their collection contains at least something for just about every imaginable country and century. However, they are strongest in certain parts of their collection:

- Records for the early nineteenth century and eighteenth and seventeenth centuries.

- Records of birth and marriage rather than death.

- Records from the countries from which the majority of Mormons draw their ancestors. These are the US, Canada, and the UK.

There is one crucial weakness to the Mormon collection in that virtually everything available online has been typed in by someone, often an amateur, and there is ample scope for mistakes. Beware! Mistakes of every sort imaginable abound in the IGI.

There is also massive duplication, so the same event might be listed half a dozen times.

Using the Mormon records *and no other records* with a family living in a part of the world where their coverage is good is often enough to trace a line which has already reached the mid-nineteenth century back another five generations or 150 years. This will take you back from the present through perhaps ten generations or 300 years. The Mormon records of the IGI are therefore the single most important source of genealogical information.

Note that in order to use the records of the IGI there is no registration process, so the Mormons do not have information about who is searching their databases, and you will not be contacted by them about genealogy or as a target for their evengelism. Your anonymity is preserved. The Mormons do have regional libraries which enable access to their databases. They are staffed by specialist librarians who have knowledge of how the database is structured and can give help with search queries in order to maximise your chance of success. These librarians are predominantly volunteers who are members of the Mormon faith, and there are stories of librarians seeking to evangelise visitors.

ACTIVITY

Discover the most important single website
Go to the most important single site for internet genealogy:
http://www.familysearch.org (see Figure 5).

Have you traced your family far enough back to find ancestors in the Mormon records? There are plenty of records before the mid nineteenth century, as well as some later. If yes, great. If no, you need more work in other records, detailed in this *How To* guide. Read on.

ACTIVITY

Working with the IGI advanced search

The entry screen on the IGI website offers you a basic search facility. This might be all you need to search for an ancestor. At one extreme, your ancestor may have a name so unusual that you can type it in, press search, and the IGI will retrieve a handful of relevant records based on a global search. More commonly a reasonably unusual name, plus, for example, a date of birth may well produce the required record.

However, you will soon find the basic search frustrating, and my advice is to move quickly to the advanced search. Almost always you are better using the advanced search as the basic search is just too basic to give useful results.

The minimum information you must enter is your ancestor's first name and surname. But usually you will need to specify an event (birth, marriage or death) and an approximate year, as well as a place where the event took place. And it is possible to refine further with parents' names or spouse's name.

The IGI has many, many quirks. The ones you need to know about are as follows:

1. The IGI is full of errors. Data is entered without checking, often by amateurs. You should regard everything you find as requiring further checking.

2. Even the framework of the IGI is faulty. For example, its list of English counties contains some in recognisable but nonetheless garbled forms. The county of Gloucestershire does not appear, though Gloucester and Gloster do, and both refer to the county and not the town.

3. You can restrict your search to a region (eg British Isles), a country (eg Scotland) and a county (eg Lothian), but that is it. You cannot in any simple way search just one parish or a group of parishes. If you are searching for a common name this may well be a problem.

4. Records on the IGI are entered in batches. A typical batch is all the christenings from a particular parish. If you know the batch number it is possible to enter this, and so search only for a certain batch of records. The problem is finding the batch numbers, and for these the IGI is not an easy source. Rather Google 'free IGI batch numbers' for sites that are offering just this information. Several of these exist.

5. One of the most satisfying IGI searches is for all children of named parents, a so-called 'parent search'. This picks up brothers and sisters whose existence you may otherwise have known nothing of. Such a search is so simple to do that it is actually counter-intuitive. What you must do is enter the first name and surname of the father, the first name of the mother, and absolutely nothing else. Do not enter a country or a date range, or specify birth records, or suggest a name for the children. The system searches the whole world and all ages for children of the parents whose names you enter, and amazingly usually comes up with a list of manageable size.

4

Using Census Records

Most countries conduct a periodic survey of their population for the purposes of providing services, planning future development, and sometimes for taxation. Typically such censuses have taken place every ten years. England has the earliest surviving census in the Doomsday Book (1087). A perceived religious restriction on counting the military strength of a nation discouraged further censuses.

WHAT ARE CENSUS RECORDS?

Census records are a house-by-house document, therefore showing people living in household and family groups. They provide a lot of genealogical information very quickly, and can also provide enough detail to bring a family to life.

One problem is that a secrecy pledge usually attaches to records that are less than 100 years old. Genealogists must find their way back around a hundred years before they can access an appropriate census. Censuses before around 1840 do not exist in most countries. The census is therefore an aid primarily for ancestors who lived during the second half of the nineteenth century and in the very early twentieth century. However, this includes ancestors who were old at the time of the earliest census, and children at the time of the last census available, so you might be lucky and find someone born as early as the mid eighteenth century on an early census, while it is just about possible for someone on the more recent census released to be alive today.

The original census records were indexed house-by-house. In order to find a record quickly, it was once necessary to know the exact address of your ancestors at a given date. As this information is often not known, searching the census used to be a very slow process indeed. And in some jurisdictions it still is. The census records for Ireland, for example, are available sometimes on microfiche, sometimes as the original paper ledgers, and there is no indexing by name. You have to either know an exact address, or be prepared to search household by household through a village or suburb. This represents a lot of hours of work.

The good news is that many census records are now available through online databases. Sometimes these are free, sometimes there are charges – but the charges are usually very modest. All census records for England, Wales and Scotland are now covered in this way.

What you can find on a census return is typically:

- The exact address where your ancestors were living.

- The full name, age and occupation of every person living at that address, including people who are not family members.

- The relationship of each person to the head of the household.

- Frequently, the place of birth.

- Sometimes information about religion or disability.

YOUR AGE?

"Oh, just turned seventeen, if you please, sir."

PUZZLE—FIND THE CAT.

Fig. 6. Census cartoon.

ACTIVITY

Locate census records

Find the records that are important for you. Frequently, there are several websites that offer access to the same body of census material. Some are free. Some make a charge, either pay-per-record or subscription – these charges are usually low. Some of the major collections are:

UK:
www.familyrecords.gov.uk/frc/research/censusmain.htm
www.nationalarchives.gov.uk/census/
www.censusuk.co.uk
www.1911census.co.uk
www.scotlandspeople.gov.uk

US:
http://www.census-online.com/links/

CANADA:
http://www.census-online.com/links/Canada/

AUSTRALIA:
http://www.coraweb.com.au/census.htm/

Otherwise, try Google – country name plus 'census' should turn up records.

YEARS CENSUSES ARE AVAILABLE FOR

In the British Isles, censuses are available to search for the following years: 1841, 1851, 1861, 1871, 1881, 1891, 1901, 1911. The 1911 census became available in 2009, two years earlier than generally expected and two years before the one-hundred year pledge of secrecy given when it was taken expired. There is effectively no access to the 1921 or later censuses. Very rarely permission to see a record may be granted within the context of a freedom of information request, but the process is expensive, slow and unwieldy, and not an online process. Basically, forget about 1921 or subsequent census records.

Prior to 1841, there were numerical censuses every ten years from 1801 – counts of people without names (though the surname of the head of household was recorded) or much other information.

These can very occasionally provide some genealogical information, but are not available online. There are also a handful of fragments prior to 1841 where more information was taken and preserved. But for all practical purposes, the census for British genealogists starts in 1841.

INFORMATION ON CENSUSES

The information given on all censuses 1851 to 1911 is very similar. For each address you will find the name of everyone who lives there. Additional information for each individual is age, occupation and place of birth. Each household has a 'head', and everyone else is described in terms of their relationship to the 'head'. Typically this information is in the form 'wife', 'son', 'daughter', 'mother-in-law'; also 'visitor', 'lodger', 'servant'.

The 1841 census is rather sparser with information. It gives age only to the nearest five years (additionally usually but not always the precise age for children) and for place of birth it asks only whether born in the same county. Often it appears that the enumerator guessed the age of people.

ACCURACY OF CENSUSES

For all censuses 1841 to 1901, the accuracy of the information depends both on what a household member told the census official, and how carefully that official wrote it down. Often only the first names and surnames of people are given, with the middle names simply left out. Occasionally, you find just initials plus surnames, reflecting an age which considered first names to be a private matter and chose not to share them with the census official. Places of birth are often places that would not have been familiar to the census official, and are typically spelt as they were heard. When people were born well away from their place of residence, there was a tendency to give just a broad area rather than a precise place. Thus London census returns are full of people born just in 'Scotland' – the census enumerator should have written down the exact parish and the county in Scotland, but often didn't do this. Ages are frequently wrong, perhaps through muddle, perhaps through a genuine reluctance to tell the official. Occupations vary enormously – you might find someone describing themselves precisely as say 'farmer of 75 acres employing 3 men' – or you might find the briefest possible statement of occupation. The most common occupation on all the available censuses is 'Ag Lab', agricultural labourer.

The modern transcription has created another level of error. Overall, the census transcripts claim an accuracy better than 98.5%. However, the errors are most common in surnames, so the reality is that errors which cause problems are more common than the around one in a hundred errors that the transcripts achieve overall. There are a lot of number errors by transcribers – typically 4 for 9 – so a child recorded as four years old might really be nine years old.

There are certainly weaknesses in the online censuses, but overall the census records are a magnificent resource. Few documents bring families to life in the way that these records do. They list millions of individuals decade-by-decade, the richest and poorest in the country.

THE 1911 CENSUS

For most genealogists starting off in their census search, the challenge is to get back as far as the most recent released census, that of 1911. The primary records to help you on your way through the twentieth century are the records of birth, marriage and death. Once you are back as far as 1911, then searching this census is very easy. A basic search is made by surname and first name (one first name only is recommended, so ignore middle names), and if the name you are searching for is unusual this information alone will be enough to find an entry. Probably you will need to add more information. This might be year of birth (exact or a year range), place of residence, place of birth, even occupation or the names of other family members. The trick is to add as little as possible in order to get a result, as the search engine is set up so that it only finds exact matches for the information you input.

The exact matches requirement means the 1911 census index is severely unforgiving. If an ancestor's name was originally entered as 'Sophie' a search for 'Sophia' won't find her. If a birthplace was entered as 'Monkley' then the correct spelling for that Devonshire village – 'Monkleigh' – won't find it. Transcription has created an additional layer of errors. Transcribers make many mistakes. Sometimes these are easy to understand – 'Aguila' for the first name 'Aquila', or '14' for the age '19' – but at other times they are beyond understanding. It is possible to make searches of the 1911 census using wildcards and the method is described on the website, but the system is cumbersome. You may well find it easier simply to think of possible alternative spellings and try them.

You can access the index to the 1911 census for free, and this index alone will give you some information. Access to entries is through a system of 'credits' bought online from the National Archives. Basically, it costs about £1 to see a transcription of a household return, or about £3 to see a reproduction of the original page, though the credit system means that in practice modest minimum fees apply as you cannot buy access to just a single result.

The 1911 census is the only census so far released which was completed by members of the household rather than by a census enumerator. The census therefore provides a specimen of the handwriting of one person who lived in the household (often the head of household, though sometimes a more educated spouse or child) and therefore a tangible link with people from a century ago. It is very special to see a form completed in your ancestor's handwriting and signed by them.

THE 1881 CENSUS

The other censuses 1841–1901 have search systems which are far more user-friendly. The greatest census asset for genealogists is the 1881 census, which is both beautifully indexed and available for free.

The search system for pre-1911 censuses is one where you enter as much information as you have, and the search engine provides ranked results. It is not based on exact matches. Very often the entry you want will be top of the list, and almost always it will be towards the top. The search mechanism deals with variants of names, deals with inaccurate dates, deals with spelling errors – in a nutshell it does your work for you.

ACTIVITY

Searching the census
▶ This is the core of much of your genealogical searching, yet it can be set out in a sentence: search the census online for your ancestors.

▶ Start with the 1911 and 1881 census returns. Use others to fill the gaps. Use 1841 last.

▶ Very often you can trace an ancestor on a census in every decade of their life. It is possible for an ancestor born say 1840 to show up on eight census returns.

▶ Remember to have a look at neighbours in the same street or village. This gives an idea of the sort of community in which your ancestor was living.

▶ Institutions (hospitals, work-house, hotels, ships, barracks) all made census returns, and can provide useful information.

5

Other Major Sources

Once you have a basic family tree worked out, you will want to find your way to other sources. A massive source of information – and amazingly one compiled by an amateur with support from amateur volunteers – is Cyndi's List.

CYNDI'S LIST

Sooner or later every genealogist will find their way to Cyndi's List: http://www.cyndislist.com (see Figure 7). This is a site of links to genealogy resources worldwide. What makes it unbeatable is its size – well over 250,000 links to sites and fast growing. Since 1996, Cyndi's List has been a major starting point for genealogy, and it is now entrenched as a key resource. The quarter of a million plus links are well indexed, so it is reasonably easy to find what might be of use to you. You can look, for example, by location, by religion, by occupation, or by a wealth of other categories. There is a line or two of information about each link, which should help you to decide whether it is likely to be useful before clicking. Using Cyndi's List you can overview a lot of sites very quickly.

The results are as variable as the sites to which Cyndi's List links. Some are indeed underwhelming. The majority are not primarily designed as sources for internet genealogy, but rather describe paper-based records, or have genealogical information as a by-product of their main function. For example, if you want to find the address of a particular record office, along with telephone number and opening hours, Cyndi's List will probably take you there. If you want to find a modern community website, Cyndi's List will have information. A minority of links lead through to databases which can be used directly for genealogy on the internet – yet a minority of 250,000 is still many thousands of sites.

Cyndi's List is best used as a site to browse when you have the framework of a family tree. Background information can be accessed from it very well. For example, if you want a map of the locality in which your ancestor lived around the time your ancestor lived there, Cyndi's List can probably help. If your ancestor was a glover or a yeoman and you want to understand these occupations, again Cyndi's List works. For more precise information you might be lucky – it is worthwhile looking.

ACTIVITY

Countries on Cyndi's List

This guide is geared towards the genealogy of English-speaking countries, but maybe your ancestor is from another country. Cyndi's List is the easiest way to find out just what is available – just go to the appropriate country page. These are the sort of questions you can answer with Cyndi:

▶ Where are the birth, marriage and death (BMD) records/vital records for a country? Are they online?

▶ Where are the census records for a country? Are they online?

▶ What is the extent of the International Geneaological Index (IGI) (Mormon) coverage of a country?

▶ What else exists?

Google™

○ Web ⦿ CyndisList.com   [Search]

1996-2009: Your genealogy starting point online for more than a decade!

264,040+ links for family history!

Main Category Index

A B C D E F G H I J K L M N O P Q R S T U V W

255,210 in 180+ categories, 8,830+ new and uncategorized

Browse Cyndi's List:
- Main Index
- Topical Index
- Alphabetical Index
- "No Frills" Index
- Text-Only Index

Search:
- Search or Browse

Browse New Links submitted in:
- March
- February
- January
- ...and more

Submit a New Link

Mailing List
- Browse Archives
- Search Archives
- RSS Archives

Cyndi's List Blog

🔲 SHARE ▪ 🔖 ✉ ...

Find us on Facebook

About Cyndi's List

Acadian, Cajun & Creole *(106)*
Updated January 24, 2009

Adoption *(192)*
Updated January 25, 2009

Africa *(209)*
Updated January 20, 2009

African-American *(649)*
Updated February 7, 2009

Ancestry.com: The Basics *(166)*
Updated August 18, 2007

Asia & The Pacific *(443)*
Updated February 16, 2009

Australia *(1161)*
Updated January 20, 2009

Austria / Österreich *(241)*
Updated January 20, 2009

The Baltic States ~ Estonia, Latvia & Lithuania *(189)*
Updated January 20, 2009

Baptist *(115)*
Updated June 8, 2007

Beginners *(158)*
Updated January 24, 2009

Belgium / Belgique / België *(157)*
Updated January 24, 2009

Biographies *(229)*
Updated January 20, 2009

Births & Baptisms *(464)*
Updated February 16, 2009

Blogs for Genealogy *New!* *(95)*
Updated February 6, 2009

Books *(411)*
Updated January 24, 2009

Calendars & Dates *(138)*
Updated January 27, 2009

Newspapers *(709)*
Updated March 7, 2009

New Zealand *(274)*
Updated January 24, 2009

Norway / Norge *(331)*
Updated January 25, 2009

Novelties *(65)*
Updated January 25, 2009

Numbering Systems *(33)*
Updated December 14, 2008

Obituaries *(571)*
Updated January 25, 2009

Occupations *(355)*
Updated February 17, 2009

Occupations - Entertainment *New!*
(72)
Updated April 27, 2008

Odds & Ends *(60)*
Genealogy Web Site Awards; Surveys, Polls & Statistics; This & That
Updated July 12, 2008

Oral History & Interviews *(109)*
Updated December 27, 2008

Organizing Your Research *(58)*
Updated January 24, 2009

Orphans *(146)*
Updated June 22, 2008

Passports *(49)*
Updated June 21, 2008

PDAs & Handhelds *(50)*
Updated November 24, 2008

Personal Home Pages *(10163)*
Alphabetical by the TITLE of the site
Updated March 7, 2009
A, B, C, D, E, F, G, H, I, J, K, L, M, N, O, P, Q, R, S, T, U, V, W, X, Y, Z

---

http://www.cyndislist.com/   10/03/2009

Fig. 7. Cyndi's List.

Cyndi and solutions for problems

Maybe you've got this far without problems. Your ancestors have been found in BMD and census records, and with the Mormon records you are busy tracing a line back to Adam and Eve.

But probably you have problems. Everyone does. Maybe you are looking for records in an unusual jurisdiction and cannot locate the records. Maybe your ancestor really was called John Smith, and there are hundreds by this name born every year. Maybe your ancestors emigrated, changed their names and hid their past.

There is a way forward.

▶ Write down the problem. For example, my ancestor was Jewish and changed his name when he came to Britain.

▶ Now express the problem using keywords: Jewish, Jewish surnames, name-change, immigration.

▶ Search or browse Cyndi's List using these key words.

RELIGIOUS COLLECTIONS

In past ages, it was religious institutions that were foremost in recording information about the lives of everyday people, and collections are built around the prevalent religion of the community. So for eighteenth century England the state religion was the Church of England, and that Church was responsible for most record keeping. Any ancestor who did not conform with the dominant religion of their time and location is likely to be treated differently in the records. Unfortunately, this often also means they will be less well recorded, or that the records are harder to find.

Some of the biggest religious collections relate to the Jewish faith. These tend to be on a country-by-country basis.

Nonconformist ancestors
- ▶ Do you have non-conformist ancestors?
- ▶ How was their faith received within the community in which they lived? Tolerated? Persecuted?
- ▶ Find what records there are. Cyndi's List is once again a great starting point.

REGIONAL COLLECTIONS

Be aware that a lot of conventional, paper-based records are in regional offices and libraries, often very small collections. More often than not these records are not available online – in many cases, even the index is not online. Sometimes record office staff will carry out short searches for you, occasionally for free, usually at a small charge. However, the trend worldwide is for most offices to provide a list of commercial genealogists who can undertake work for you, which is rarely a cheap solution.

For the internet genealogist, the solution is Look-up Exchanges.

Find local record offices
In most parts of the world, local record offices are linked to the national library service, and the collections are often held as part of that library's resources. You really need a standard Google search to find what may be available. You might find a super collection, or nothing.

LOOK-UP EXCHANGES

This is a system where you email a request to someone who looks for you in a paper-based resource. This might be their local record office, or perhaps in a specialised directory they have on their bookshelf. The system envisages that you will look-up something for them as an exchange, or offer something else.

Britain is full of these exchanges. There are hundreds and hundreds of them. Elsewhere they seem very scarce. Certainly they do exist in the US, Commonwealth countries and elsewhere, but in nothing like the British profusion.

ACTIVITY

Ask someone!
First, find a look-up exchange:

UK: http://www.ukgenealogy.co.uk/lookup.htm/

Anywhere else: http://www.cyndislist.com/lookups.htm

Then decide what you are going to offer in exchange:

▶ Information. If you have access to paper records which interest the other party or if they are interested in your research this is the simplest solution.

▶ Money. Quite a few people offering their services in look-up exchanges are in fact freelance genealogists taking advantage of free advertising.

▶ A charity donation. A lot of amateurs would be very happy to see their time rewarded by you giving a small sum to a charity.

▶ Your thanks. That's all a lot of enthusiasts want.

FINDING RELATIVES

Finding relatives through traditional, pre-internet genealogy was difficult. The process of moving forward from an ancestor to children and grandchildren, finding someone who is alive today and tracking them down was possible, but it was slow and full of frustrations. The records are simply not designed to be used in this way.

The process of finding relatives alive today whom you once knew and with whom you have lost contact is an area where the web is strong. Even a simple Google search may work, or there are numerous person finder services. For more distant links, as ever, it is the internet to the rescue! The basic idea is that you enter details of an ancestor, and find other people – your cousins – who are descended from the same person.

Alternatively, you can search for a single-name study. This is a project where someone is trying to produce a comprehensive family tree of everyone who bears a particular surname. Surname studies work best with unusual surnames, though even common surnames are possible when the name is studied in conjunction with a location.

ACTIVITY

Getting in touch
Start with the two (linked) big websites.

FriendsReunited is the pre-eminent person finder indexed on area, school and university: http://www.friendsreunited.com/

GenesReunited is the best way to find descendants of a named ancestor. A fast growing site at: http://www.genesreunited.com/

Try to find a single-name study. Google is unbeatable – enter the surname you are interested in and 'single name study' – and try also 'surname study'. If you can connect with a well-researched family you have hit the genealogical jackpot, and will discover relatives galore!

PAY SITES

With so much available on the internet for free, the pay sites can only exist by offering something extra. Typically, they have massive databases and powerful search engines.

The initial check has to be that they really are providing added value. There are scams out there. A simple search for the 1881 census reveals several sites that charge for information from this census, yet the 1881 census is available for free. Several sites sell birth, marriage and death certificates at higher prices than those charged by the official GRO – and these sites simply buy the certificates from the GRO. It is very hard to see what added value sites such as these are giving.

Approach pay sites with caution – but note that there really is good material available for a fee.

ACTIVITY

Pay sites
Payment can either be on a pay-per-view basis, or on the basis of a monthly subscription. You can expect to find useful material on the pay sites, though much of it can be found for free with a little persistence.

▶ Consider what sort of payment plan suits you. Some have free introductory offers or discounted packages for new members.

▶ Think about what site you want to use. Two big ones are: www.ancestry.com (US and worldwide) and www.1837on-line.com/ (UK).

6

Military

In the nineteenth century and the first half of the twentieth century, very many men had a period of military service. A few women also served, particularly as nurses. An enormous and often complex body of records relate to military service. Records relating to the First World War are the most accessible. The many conflicts of the nineteenth century have all left an impressive body of records.

MILITARY RECORDS

Military records come in two broad categories:

- records of individuals;

- records of a military unit in which an individual served.

Records of individuals who may still be alive have restrictions governing access. If you want to find the record of an individual who served in the Second World War, almost certainly you will find it is classified. If the record relates to you, then in theory you should be able to gain access to it under freedom of information legislation, though the process is exceptionally bureaucratic. First World War records are in the process of becoming available, but even here many nations are still applying pledges given many years ago to restrict access. Individuals' records (when they are

Fig. 8. First World War medal card search screen.

51

available) have the potential to be very interesting but often disappoint by their brevity. Medal cards are the starting point for British and Commonwealth First World War records, using the National Archives' search system as shown in Figure 8. The main exception is records of those who died while serving.

Records relating to a military unit can be far more satisfying. You do need precise information – for example, both regiment name and battalion – in order to access such records. However, the reward can be a wealth of detail, potentially even daily diary entries of activities. You are most unlikely to find a record of your ancestor by name.

ACTIVITY

Commonwealth War Graves Commission

Search the Commonwealth War Graves Commission site (see Figure 9). This is a top-quality resource listing the 1.7 million men and women of the Commonwealth forces who died during the two world wars – along with the 23,000 cemeteries, memorials and other locations worldwide where they are commemorated. The register can also be searched for details of the 67,000 Commonwealth civilians who died as a result of enemy action in the Second World War. The information given is not uniform, but tends to be reasonably full, typically name, rank, home address, next of kin and exact place of burial – often with photographs of the appropriate cemetery. See: http://www.cwgc.org

ACTIVITY

Regimental histories

Find a regimental history. If a regiment exists today, it will have a website which will contain at least an outline history and information about battle honours. Many old regiments have been merged, but the successor regiment will remember all its source regiments. Most

:: CWGC ::

CWGC
Commonwealth War Graves Commission

Search our Records

Help

Common Questions

Who We Are

What We Do

Histories

News and Events

Audio – Video

Publications

Education

Contact Us

Information and Service

Debt of Honour Register

Search for — Casualty

Surname

Initials

War

Year of death — From / To

Force

Nationality — of the force served

Submit

Welcome

The "Debt of Honour Register" is the Commission's database listing the 1.7 million men and women of the Commonwealth forces who died during the two world wars and the 23,000 cemeteries, memorials and other locations worldwide where they are commemorated. The register can also be searched for details of the 67,000 Commonwealth civilians who died as a result of enemy action in the Second World War.

Place mouse over 🛈 button for more information about the particular field.

Searches are *not* case sensitive. Search criteria may be entered in upper, lower or mixed case. Searches are *not* phonetic. The search will not find names that sound similar to the one you have entered.

Home | Site Map | Contact Us | Links | Search our Records | Privacy Policy | Ts & Cs | Credits | Accessibility

10/03/2009

http://www.cwgc.org/debt_of_honour.asp?menuid=14

Fig. 9. Commonwealth War Graves Commission search screen.

regiments have a regimental museum. These are rich sources for information about life in the regiment at the time, and the activities of the regiment. There seems to be no online key to regimental sites worldwide, so it is a Google search for the regiment name. Among the results, you need to distinguish between official and unofficial sites. For genealogists useful material is usually only in the official sites, as the unofficial sites tend to cover only very recent history.

ACTIVITY

Battle of the Somme

View an example of a First World War battle with a substantial web presence.

See: http://www.bbc.co.uk/history/war/wwone/battle_ somme.shtml

7

Wills and Where to Find them Online

This is a new and developing area of the internet. Not long ago searching for wills meant a painstaking search through numerous repositories containing records from a frequently non-intuitive catchment area. Whole books have been written on locating wills. Now the online position is far from perfect, but it is improving.

THE PROBLEM WITH WILLS

Wills are among the most interesting genealogical documents. Unfortunately, many wills tend to be stored at local level rather than in national repositories, and the indexes are only just coming online. Progress is being made with internet listing for the earlier wills – generally eighteenth century and before – for example, many English, Welsh and Scottish wills can now be downloaded. Unfortunately, the coverage of online sources is still patchy and for most internet genealogists wills remain a frustrating area.

ACTIVITY

Thinking about wills
If you are searching for ancestors in England and Wales, check out: http://www.familyrecords.gov.uk/topics/wills.htm. Otherwise see if Cyndi's List has online suggestions for the state or county in question.

8

Migration

People have always moved around.

The British Isles have traditionally been an area from which people emigrated. Your Victorian relative who just vanishes without a trace probably emigrated, and it may be that you could pick them up in America, Canada, Australia, New Zealand, South Africa, or another part of the British Empire. Migration into Britain has been commonplace since the 1950s, but relatively rare before then. Notwithstanding there were migrants from the European continent, or reverse migrants from a part of the British Empire.

IMMIGRATION AND EMIGRATION

Every country has its own, special collections, and you will gradually become familiar with these. For example, for anyone living in the New World, sooner or later immigration records are going to be essential.

Records of twentieth century migrations from Africa, the Caribbean and Asia to Europe and North America are a problematic area – records are scant and many of the records which exist are too recent to have been released. In Britain some help is available at: www.movinghere.org.uk – I am not aware of a comparable North American site.

ACTIVITY

Passenger arrival lists

Very many immigrants to the US passed through New York's Ellis Island on their way to a new life. Most records are available online.

Ellis Island Records are both a genealogical resource and a key record of the development of the US. For anyone of any nation (with or without US migrants among their ancestors) this is a fascinating site. See: http://www.ellisisland.org

9

Newspapers

One of the hardest sources for the genealogist to access is newspapers. Old newspapers in theory contain a phenomenal amount of information for genealogists. The problem is that as most lack indexes, this information is practically unsearchable. Very slowly some information from old newspapers is becoming available through the internet – so far mainly the obituaries in major, national papers.

WHAT NEWSPAPERS OFFER

Because the vast majority of newspapers have no indexing whatsoever, it is still very hard to find material of genealogical interest. Searching even a week of newspapers for reference to an ancestor is a laborious undertaking.

But there is some good news.

The Times newspaper is indexed. There are index books for *The Times* which are still found in many British public libraries. They are practical to use if you can date an event at least to within a few years. However, the most exciting development is that *The Times* has been digitised and may now be searched either on dvd or online. This is a subscription service. Individuals are unlikely to get enough use from it to justify paying for a subscription, which is expensive, but the larger public libraries do have access to it. It offers full text, facsimiles of every page as published from more than two hundred years of *The Times* (London), fully searchable by keywords. The index covers everything, including obituaries, family announcements and business advertisements. This last area is a most useful source for the genealogist. It is as simple as making a Google style search. You may be lucky enough to find a reference to your ancestor by name in *The Times*. More probably you will find reference to activities your ancestor is linked with. For example movements of regiments and ships are well recorded.

Some local papers are now becoming accessible through the work of local history societies. Typically they offer pdf images of the newspaper plus an index, and often the index covers no more than a sample period of a few months or a year. You might be lucky. Anyway, this is a growing resource.

Many local newspapers today are interested in publishing old photographs, or will publish an old story relevant to the locality. This can be a great way to find out more about a picture or story, or to connect with relatives living in the locality today.

ACTIVITY

Connecting through local newspapers
Google search for an appropriate local newspaper.

Write a short letter to their letters page asking for relatives to contact you.

If your ancestor did something noteworthy, talk to a commissioning editor on the phone and suggest you write a short article. Many newspapers would be happy to publish.

An example of a family story in a newspaper article

Account from The Kent and Canterbury Press 1911

SAD END OF A CANTERBURY NEWSAGENT

BODY FOUND IN FOUR FEET OF WATER

A JURY'S INSISTENCE

INQUEST ADJOURNED FOR MEDICAL EVIDENCE

AN UNEXPECTED DEVELOPMENT

The dead body of Walter George Bates a well known Canterbury newsagent who was also employed in the leather department of Messrs Kennedy & Boot Stores, Sun Street was taken out of the river Stour early on Monday morning last. The death had the appearance of being clouded by much mystery for the man was stated to have been in good health recently and to have had no worries...

10

Occupations

A scrap of information you will find about most ancestors is their occupation. It is worthwhile trying to get as much information as you can from this.

JOB TITLES

The job titles of even a hundred years ago are very different from those of today.

By far the most common is agricultural labourer – usually recorded simply as 'Ag Lab'. This refers to a manual labourer on a farm, and was a hard and lowly-paid job. Also common is general labourer – 'Gen Lab' – which is a manual labourer within an urban setting, and can refer to a factory worker, a railway or dockyard worker, or a host of other labouring occupations.

In the countryside the old social divisions were preserved well into the nineteenth century. The key occupation is Yeoman, someone who farmed rented land. The freeholder of the land was likely to be a Gentleman. Working either for the Yeoman or directly for the Gentleman landowner were such occupations as husbandman, grazier and shepherd. The majority of workers in the country were agricultural labourers. Rural life was supported by such occupations as millers, bakers, butchers, innkeepers and shopkeepers.

In the towns an enormous number of occupations are found. While some are familiar, many occupations are simply not found today. A real effort is needed to understand what your ancestor's job really was.

ACTIVITY

Understand your ancestor's job
A list (UK themed) is at: http://web.ukonline.co.uk/thursday. handleigh/ demography/occupations-wages-money/old-occupations/oldocc-c.htm

There is a short list (American themed) at: http://www.usgenweb.org/ research/occupations.shtml

The Poor and Workhouse Records

Most families were dependent on money from the poor law at some time. Throughout the nineteenth century, the poor law was administered as part of the workhouse system. While some workhouses were better than others, many were every bit as bleak and depressing as that portrayed in Charles Dickens's *Oliver Twist*. In the eighteenth century, the poor were supported within their parish, and there was the concept of 'settlement' within a specific parish. Someone away from the place of their birth who needed help would be resettled back to their parish of birth.

RECORDS OF THE POOR

Most people were poor. Almost certainly the majority of ancestors you discover will be poor. The overwhelming majority of people who emigrated from Europe did so to escape poverty and for those who remained, Europe was indeed characterised by what America saw as huddled masses of poor and oppressed.

ACTIVITY

Understanding nineteenth century poverty
This is of course a vast area of social history – but you can explore some of the themes. Wikipedia is a good jumping off point. For example:
The English Poor Law:

http://en.wikipedia.org/wiki/Poor_Law

Hobos in the USA:
http://en.wikipedia.org/wiki/Hobo

Swagmen in Australia:
http://en.wikipedia.org/wiki/Swagman

12

Noble Ancestors

Just as everyone has poor ancestors, so too everyone has noble ancestors. Within the British Isles and for people whose ancestry goes back to the British Isles, everyone is (distantly) related to the Queen. It is just that not everyone knows exactly who their noble ancestors are, or precisely how they are related to the Queen – but I'm quite sure she is a relative, and you should be also!

FINDING NOBLE ANCESTORS

Of course many families record stories of links with the aristocracy. It may be that a reputed link with a noble family has motivated your genealogical quest. Such stories can be great fun, and they may even be correct. Very often, however, they are confused somewhere through the generations of re-telling. As with all family research, you have to start with what you know and go back from there – you cannot jump to the noble line mentioned and find a line going forward.

The great bonus of actually finding a link with an aristocratic family is that you will find people who have left records, and whose lives you can find far more about than the bare bones of birth, marriage and death. Noble ancestors are fun.

What you are looking for is called a 'gateway' ancestor. This is someone who is a known member of an established genealogy and can link you to a rich heritage.

Even if you have no family tradition of links with the aristocracy, you can be sure that those links will be there, somewhere. Imagine a child born in your family in the year 2000. That child has two parents, four grandparents, and eight great-grand-parents. Assuming as a rule of thumb three generations in a century, then that child's eight great-grandparents were born around 1900.

Going back another century gives 16 great-great-grandparents, 32 great-great-great-grandparents, and 64 great-great-great-great-grandparents – born around 1800.

Another three generations produces 512 direct ancestors by 1700.

4,096 by 1600.

32,768 by 1500.

262,144 by 1400.

2,097,152 by 1300.

Every one of us has in excess of two-million direct ancestors born around 700 years ago – excluding of course the reduction through marriages of cousins. That's a lot of people. If you are tracing a line in Britain, then two-million people in Britain in 1300 is more than the population of the country at that time. Basically in Britain everyone who can establish a line back more than a couple of generations is related to everyone else. Our neighbours are also our relatives. And everyone will have a drop of blue blood somewhere. There is even a massive multi-volume book – *The Plantagenet Roll of the Blood Royal* – which seeks to list all known descendants of the Plantagenet kings.

If you do find a link to a noble family you will find your research has in effect been done already. And within the European tradition every noble family is ultimately related to every other noble family. Find just about any noble ancestor in your line and you can claim as a relative the Queen of England, the King of Spain, the King of Belgium – even the last Tsar of Russia or the last Kaiser of Germany. The European nobility is one big family.

TITLES AND COATS OF ARMS

Within Europe, titles descend through families following strict rules. The European tradition is for titles to pass from father to eldest son, so the system discriminates both on order of birth and on gender. Finding an ancestor who is titled is most unlikely to give you the right to a title.

Coats of arms are more complex. In the British Isles, all titled families have a coat of arms, but not all families with a coat of arms have a title.

A WARNING!

There are plenty of companies that will try to sell you a shield, coat of arms or similar which they say belongs to your ancestor's surname. This just isn't correct. Coasts of arms belong only to individuals, never to surnames, and are granted to specific individuals only by the appropriate legal system in each of the European countries. Through a process of registration in each generation they can be inherited by descendants of the first bearer, sometimes with modifications. That someone bearing your surname had a right to a coat of arms gives you no right whatsoever to that coat of arms, and indeed if you use it (for example, on a letter heading) then you are committing an offence and could in theory face prosecution.

Most surnames are older than coats of arms. A particular surname may well be associated with individuals who have completely different coats of arms. For example, the surname 'Norton' has at least a dozen different coats of arms associated with it, and if you or your ancestor has the surname Norton there is no reason to assume you are descended from someone entitled to any one of these coats of arms.

If you really do like the idea of a coat of arms you do of course have the option of registering one in your own name. The College of Arms (for England, Wales and Northern Ireland) or the Court of Lord Lyon (for Scotland) will both design and register a coat of arms for you. There is information on their websites. If you are an upstanding British national, you can (on payment of several thousand pounds) have designed and registered a coat of arms, which in time can pass to your children (who will have to pay a modest registration fee).

Titles are not as easy to acquire. However, the English title 'Lord of the Manor' relates to ownership of a particular piece of property. This may be a manor house, or the title may be attached to a field which has a relatively low value. It is even possible for the title today to relate solely to a bundle of legal papers. The title 'Lord of the Manor' can be bought and sold, and at any time there are usually a few on the market. The Scottish title 'Laird' is a courtesy title with no legal status, so in theory anyone may decide to call themselves 'laird'. In reality, certain long-established estates have the title attached to them, and 'laird' in effect means the owner of a particular estate.

ACTIVITY

Heraldry and genealogy

▶ If your ancestor had a coat of arms, the court of arms in the relevant jurisdiction will have records of grant and inheritance. Contact them.

▶ Coats of arms are still being granted by European courts. If you are an upstanding citizen of a European country which has an extant arms system (or you can establish a connection) you can petition the appropriate body for a new grant of arms – for you and your descendants. The present cost in England is in the region of £5,000.

▶ The two bodies you are most likely to use are: The College of Arms (England and Wales, plus Northern Ireland and Commonwealth) www.college-of-arms.gov.uk and Court of the Lord Lyon (Scotland) www.lyon-court.com.

A NOTE ON TITLES

Broadly there are three types:

■ Inherited titles: Duke, Earl, Marquis, Viscount, Baron – the real nobility.

■ Baronets, and life peerages.

■ Titles which belong to the owner of a piece of land, such as Lord of the Manor (in England) and Laird (in Scotland).

The title you are most likely to come across is Baronet. For hundreds of years, this has been effectively the entry level title. Today it is a life peerage, but until recently it was awarded as an hereditary title.

13

Directories

Our modern telephone directories are part of a tradition going back more than two-hundred years of compiling lists of people who live in a locality. While never comprehensive, they have often covered high proportions of people, and can give useful information.

WORKING WITH DIRECTORIES

For the second half of the twentieth century, the standard type of directory was the telephone directory. Most people who lived at this time in developed countries are likely to be in a telephone directory. Most old British telephone directories are now available and fully searchable (through http://www.ancestry.co.uk, on payment of a subscription) and can be useful for tracking down recent ancestors. By contrast, for the period around 1850–1950, the standard directories are trade directories. Generally, these were produced annually for every city and town. Typically they give information of three sorts:

1. Background information about the town, often in a very formal style. Typically trade directories give such information as population size, transport links, markets, closing days, churches, schools. This might help to provide some context for one of your ancestors. It might also include a reference to one

	Title	Location	Decade	Key name	
Home	Kelly's Directory of Kent, 1913. [Part 2: Private Resident & Trade Directories]	Kent	1910s	Kelly	Directory	Fact File
How to use this site					
Find by location	Kelly's Directory of Kent, 1913. [Part 1: County & Localities]	Kent	1910s	Kelly	Directory	Fact File
Find by decade					
Find by keywords					
About our project	Kelly's Directory of Kent, 1903. [Part 2: Private Resident & Trade Directories]	Kent	1900s	Kelly	Directory	Fact File
News & publicity					
History notes					
Site Map	Kelly's Directory of Kent, 1903. [Part 1: County & Localities]	Kent	1900s	Kelly	Directory	Fact File
	Post Office Directory of Essex, Herts, Kent ... , 1855. [Part 2: Court & Trade Directories]	Essex Hertfordshire Kent Middlesex Surrey Sussex	1850s	Post Office	Directory	Fact File
	Post Office Directory of Essex, Herts, Kent ... , 1855. [Part 1: Counties & Localities]	Essex Hertfordshire Kent Middlesex Surrey Sussex	1850s	Post Office	Directory	Fact File
	Kelly's Directory of Kent, Surrey & Sussex, 1891. [Part 2. Kent: Court & Trade Directories]	Kent	1890s	Kelly	Directory	Fact File
	Kelly's Directory of Kent, Surrey & Sussex, 1891. [Part 1. Kent: County & Localities]	Kent	1890s	Kelly	Directory	Fact File
	Melville & Co.'s Directory of	Kent	1850s	Melville	

Fig. 10. Historical Directories – example for the county of Kent.

of your ancestors in the context of this formal information – perhaps listed as magistrate, school-master or vicar.

2. Information about traders. Almost everyone who owned or managed a business, however small, will be listed. This includes, for example, the shopkeepers: greengrocers, butchers, bakers, and the like. Many people of modest means are included in the trade directories because they were traders.

3. Information about prominent residents. Many people choose to pay a modest fee to have their name and address included.

A few directories are available on the internet. The whole collection will be available at large libraries in the area, which is fine if you can visit. In theory the worldwide inter-library loan system means that you should be able to request from your local library a copy of any book – and trade directories are books – and all for a nominal administrative charge. In practice, many directories may be treated by their home library as reference only, and the heavy weight of the typical directory discourages libraries from transporting them as inter-library loans.

ACTIVITY

Directories

The electronic age has come to the rescue:

▶ There are now (incomplete) lists of the directories that exist.
▶ A few directories are available online, as, for example, shown in Figure 10.
▶ You can track down directories to buy.
▶ Some are available as pdf files.

To find directories, try the following:

A list of US directories and their locations is at:
http://www.uscitydirectories.com

A few US directories are available in pdf from:
http://www.nsbjd.com/dirlist.htm

Many US directories can be bought on microfilm from:
http://www.galegroup.com

For Canada, the recommended directory site is:
http://www.tpl.toronto.on.ca/localhistory/directories1.html

Directories from all countries can be bought on eBay:
http://www.ebay.com

Prices are often modest.

For British Isles genealogy, a special source is the free cover disks on monthly family tree magazines, which over the years have covered all major British directories. You need to buy a magazine to find out from its list what was offered on the disk with past issues, then either buy a back issue from the publisher or find the appropriate issue on eBay.

14

School and University Records

School records are not particularly well preserved, nor are they easy to search, but you may be lucky. Very few are so far online. University records are far more extensive, and some of these are online.

SCHOOLS

Most children in Victorian Britain and many in earlier ages went to school. Only at the end of the Victorian period was schooling made free and compulsory, yet well before this most benefited either from reasonably cheap schools or from charitable organisations. You are very likely to find children at school recorded on the census with the occupation 'scholar' or simply 'school'.

The difficulty is finding the name of the school. If the school is a boarding school then the name of the school will be given. But very few schools were boarding schools. Many children went to small schools using rented premises and which may only have existed for a few years – schools often called 'dame schools' (because a single school mistress taught all ages) or 'penny schools' – because they charged a penny a week. Records of such schools, if they have survived, tend to be in local collections and are usually hard to find. You will be lucky indeed to find a personal record of your ancestor at such a school. Very few records of such schools are available through the internet. A simple Google search on the name of the school should identify any records that might exist.

The public and grammar schools of Britain are a different matter entirely. Many of these have a long history, often in the same building, and many exist today. The term 'public' as used in Britain means 'private' or 'independent'. They were public in the sense that they were more widely available than the alternative of home tutoring. All such schools which exist today have websites, most with a section on the history of the school, and many will direct you to a book written about the history of the school – for it seems that almost every British school in this category has at one time or another seen the need to commission a history to celebrate an anniversary. Additionally, many schools have preserved records, typically including admission details, funding, prizes won, and leaving details. The records may include punishments, sporting achievements and first destination after school. Most schools that existed during the two world wars have a memorial to alumni who died in these wars.

ACTIVITY

Schools

Information about larger schools (rather than about their pupils) is often straightforward to find.

▶ Does the school still exist? If so, it probably has a website, and if it is an old school almost certainly something about its history will be set out.

▶ The school will be listed in directories for the time. These usually give the name of the head, whether a boarding or day school, plus the age range and number of pupils.

UNIVERSITIES

Mass access to universities is a relatively recent phenomenon dating only from the 1960s. Before this time, scholarships enabled a few from modest backgrounds to benefit from a university education, though the overwhelming majority of students were from upper or upper-middle class backgrounds. If your ancestor made it to a university prior to the Second World War, there will be records available, often published in book form, often now online.

The British Isles traditionally had nowhere near the hundred plus universities that exist today. Prior to the nineteenth century, there were just seven universities: Oxford, Cambridge, St Andrews, Glasgow, Aberdeen, Edinburgh and Dublin. The nineteenth century saw the establishment of universities in the major cities, though the overall number remained small. London gained its university at this period, along with such cities as Bristol, Manchester, Leeds, Liverpool, Newcastle and Durham. While a very few women did attend universities in the late nineteenth century, universities in the nineteenth century and before were overwhelmingly male.

Documents relating to university education include matriculation (entry to university), graduation and prizes. Most university websites have information about records which are available for that university. A few are online, many are available through books, and most now offer some form of archival search (usually requiring a donation).

ACTIVITY

Finding ancestors at university

▶ Find the present-day website of the university or college. Many have been amalgamated – if you cannot find a name you are looking for, try the university that now occupies the same buildings.

▶ Identify the archivist. Usually this is someone linked to the university's library.

▶ Send an email.

15

Working with the Wider Context

Genealogy is at its best when supported by other studies. Local history is closely allied to genealogy, as people and the places where they lived are closely linked. Maps are useful supporting documents, and should be considered. The wider historical framework is also useful, and genealogy can be an interesting route into national history.

LOCAL HISTORY

People have always moved around, and you will find that some of your ancestors covered remarkable distances even in the pre-railway age. You will also find ancestors who lived their whole life in one village, and whole families tied to the land who lived for generations in a village. You may establish a deep link between your ancestors and a particular location.

Most villages in the British Isles now have one or more books written about them. Many cover a thousand years or more of local history, typically starting with the Doomsday Book, and some-times looking back still further to pre-historic, Roman, and Anglo-Saxon remains. If you find you are descended from a family rooted for some generations in a particular village, you can be confident that some of your ancestors have lived in that locality from time immemorial. Studies of the genetic profile of people in the British Isles show that the most common ethnic signature is that belonging to the pre-Roman inhabitants of Britain. Families really do take root in an area, for generations, centuries, even millennia.

Remember that information which relates specifically to the time your ancestor lived in a place is the most relevant. Try to focus on this.

ACTIVITY

Accessing local history sources

▶ Identify the present-day website of a village. Most have an 'official' site sponsored by the local council. Many have 'unofficial' sites also.

▶ Find what the website says about the history of the village – and pull out those sections which relate to the time your ancestors lived there.

▶ Identify pictures from an appropriate time frame. These might be early photographs, drawings, perhaps even a painting.

▶ Does the locality have a local history society? If so do you have a family story that might interest them, and which they might have information about?

MAPS

You need to bear in mind the contribution that maps can make to your study.

In the British Isles one of the most useful sources is maps of the counties which show their boundaries in earlier periods. Enormous changes were made to the counties of England,

Wales and Scotland in 1974, while subsequent changes and the establishment of various urban authorities have further modified our county map. On a day-to-day basis we make less and less use of the county division. In earlier times the county was a crucial geographic unit.

There were minor changes to the county boundaries throughout the Victorian age and the twentieth century, but nothing on the scale of the 1974 change. Most counties that existed in 1974 had existed for a thousand years or more and were areas with which people identified. It is hard to see the 1974 changes as anything less than an act of cultural vandalism. For almost the whole of your genealogical study, you will be dealing with the pre-1974 counties. Thus Greenwich is not part of Greater London but part of Kent; Liverpool is not part of Merseyside but part of Lancashire. The county map is replete with such curiosities as an enormous Yorkshire and a tiny Rutland, it includes oddities like the Soke of Peterborough, and even has counties with discontinuous territories marooned within another county. This is the map on which your ancestors lived.

For the periods you are most likely to be investigating, high-quality, detailed maps exist. In towns these frequently show individual houses – so you can see the ground plan of a house your Victorian ancestor lived in – while in the country, it is often able to identify the exact fields your ancestor farmed. Regrettably, almost nothing of these sources is available online, though as with everything that isn't on the internet today it is hoped that it will be there tomorrow.

GENERAL HISTORY

Reading history to supplement your understanding of events in your ancestors' lives is an interesting way of making the past relevant. Background work in history will take you well outside the area of genealogy. Themes in most people's ancestry include migration (within countries and between countries), the urban working class of the nineteenth century, social history of the poor in all countries, and military links. Changing roles of women are exemplified by family histories.

For a general online overview of a historic topic, a good starting place is usually Wikipedia.

ACTIVITY

Finding context
Within a village context you might like to try the following:

▶ Does the village have a website today? Probably it contains some local history.

▶ What buildings exist today from the time your ancestor lived there? Probably the church. Probably some other buildings. Can you find pictures of them?

▶ Who lives there today? A telephone directory is a good starting point – do you think you have relatives living there today?

▶ Has the churchyard been transcribed and made available on the internet?

ACTIVITY

Finding maps

▶ For modern maps a powerful source is Multimap at: http://www.multimap.com. The whole of Britain is covered by detailed maps.

▶ The best single source for old maps is called simply Old Maps, at: http://www.old-maps.co.uk

▶ Village websites very often include maps of their village, frequently both modern and historic.

ACTIVITY

View a timeline

A great way to get a feel for the time in which your ancestors lived is through a timeline. Try the following sites:

General timelines:
http://www.camelotintl.com/world/

Poster format timelines:
http://www.hyperhistory.com

16

Family Medical History

This is a new frontier in genealogy – whether online or offline – and one which has to be approached with caution. The idea is to understand better the genetic heritage of you and your relatives. This includes charting inherited diseases in your family.

You may find that a routine medical with your doctor will include questions about your immediate family's medical history. Questions like 'What did your parents die from?', 'Do either of your parents suffer from glaucoma?' and many similar are questions by which a doctor seeks to use family medical history to help understand the health concerns of a present family members. The most relevant people to consider for a medical history are the closest relatives.

You might like to consider compiling a specific type of genealogical record which is a Family Medical History (FMH). This type of record is gaining much support from the medical profession in the US; by contrast, in the UK there is little professional interest. Presumably this will change.

ACTIVITY

Focusing on close relatives
The closer a relative is to you, the more likely they are to offer meaningful guidance to your genetic risks. The key relatives are:
First degree: mother, father, brothers, sisters, children.

▶

Second degree: grandparent, aunts and uncles, half brothers and sisters.

Third degree: great-grandparents, great aunts and uncles, half-siblings of parents.

Beyond this there is probably little point in collecting a family medical history unless you are tracing the inheritance of a specific disease. Arguably, only first and second degree relatives are really close enough to yield much relevant information.

ACTIVITY

Identifying sources of medical information
The major sources of information are:

▶ Family knowledge.

▶ Death certificates.

▶ Hospital records.

All three are problematic. The enormous problem is that in most societies medical records are confidential, so you will find you do not have access to relatives' medical records – or even to your own record. Usually old death certificates give just an immediate cause of death rather than an underlying medical condition – recent practices in Britain have changed somewhat, but the cause of death is still usually given in just a single word or a very few words.

In view of these shortcomings family knowledge can be essential. It is important that families talk about the medical history of their relatives. However distasteful or embarrassing it might be, family members do need to know. For example, if you are a woman and have a brother or a maternal uncle who died of muscular dystrophy, then you need to know about this because you may well be a carrier of muscular dystrophy, and sons you have may well suffer from it. If you are a carrier of Tay Sachs disease, again, you need to know – if you marry someone who is also a carrier it is likely your children will have this ailment.

The area of inherited disease is of course an awkward one. When people research their family they are usually interested in knowing about the exploits of ancestors, social history, or perhaps finding noble ancestors. Finding a carrier of a terrible disease is on no one's wish list. It is rarely pleasant. I was contacted by a very distant cousin who asked, 'My immediate family suffer from familial adenomatous polyposis or FAP and my doctor has asked me to find out if relatives have it also – is this in your family?'. FAP is an inherited condition caused by a mutation of either of two genes. However, the inheritance patterns are complex and poorly understood. While the illness was not properly diagnosed until recent years, FAP has symptoms sufficiently distinctive for death certificates and family stories to suggest affected individuals. Genealogical studies can therefore provide evidence of transmission over generations, and I hope my distant relative was able to make progress for her doctor's study. On this occasion I was not able to help her as my family has escaped FAP.

The whole area of researching inherited illness is very new and very sensitive. Medical professionals would advocate that it should be discussed within the context of genetic counselling. The reality for the genealogist is that this is simply not practical. But in any event, take care!

Twins

Twins do run in families, and you may find such a tendency somewhere within your own family.

The caveat is that identical twins are not an inherited tendency, but rather it is the more common fraternal (non-identical) twins which are an inherited tendency. The tendency for giving birth to fraternal twins runs solely from mother to daughter – the male line plays no part in it. It is often possible to trace incidents of twins through several generations through the female line.

In the GRO records of birth, children are listed according to the district, volume number and page number on which their birth was recorded. Almost always the birth of twins is registered at the same time, so twins will be registered on either the same page as one another or a page with a consecutive number. Whenever you find a record of a birth, it is worth looking to see if there are children with the same surname registered on the same or consecutive pages. If there are they may well be twins.

The infant mortality rate of twins is higher than for single births, and until relatively recently much higher. Very often one of a pair of twins died shortly after birth, and as a result families may be completely unaware that a twin existed. This is something unexpected that you could discover.

Often twins are given names which are in some way pairs. Two girls might both be named after flowers blooming at the time of their birth, as Daisy and Violet. Once there was a tradition of using Aquila and Priscilla as names for twins (with either name being given to either sex) reflecting a New Testament brother and sister (though curiously not in fact twins).

LIFE EXPECTANCY

Some families consider themselves to be 'long lived' – or more rarely 'short lived'. Longevity of course depends on both genetic and environmental factors. It is indeed possible to find families that are 'long lived'.

The genetic component of longevity is the interaction of many genes rather than a single gene whose transmission can be charted. The area is exceptionally complex, and geneticists today feel that the amateur can do little. Yet genealogists do observe families which are long lived, and may even speculate on inheritance patterns. Longevity seemingly passes through the female line in families, particularly passing from mother to daughter. Many genealogies show that a woman who is long-lived has sisters, a mother, maternal grandmother, and maternal aunts and great-aunts who are all long lived. You may care to see how this maps your own family.

Curiously absence of long-lived relatives doesn't seem to preclude an individual from living a very long life.

17

DNA

DNA studies promise much and sometimes deliver, but they can also be a dead end. DNA studies can be linked with the idea of a family medical history. They can also be used with such ideas as 'Deep DNA', 'Ethnic DNA' and 'One-Name Studies'. Of one thing we can all be sure – whatever DNA can do today, it will do more tomorrow.

DNA AND INHERITED DISEASE

Many ethnic groups have a predisposition to a particular disease. For example, Tay Sachs disease is associated with the Ashkenazi Jewish population. The gene is carried by many within this population, and seems associated with an immunity from tuberculosis, actually conferring a benefit on the carrier. However, Tay Sachs disease may manifest itself in children when two carriers marry.

DNA AND FAMILY MEDICAL HISTORY

The genetic predisposition for many diseases is inherited, and by understanding the diseases members of your family have suffered from, you can gain some limited knowledge about your own genetic risks. In particular, the advantages to you are stated on numerous American health internet sites as the following:

■ Disease screening. This might be appropriate if, for example, breast cancer or colon cancer are diseases from which a relative has suffered.

■ Better prevention of diseases. For example, an oral contraceptive has some benefit in preventing ovarian cancer and may be prescribed where a risk of ovarian cancer exists.

■ Informed family planning. For example, if both parents carry the Tay Sachs gene there is a one in four chance that their child will be born with Tay Sachs disease, which is an incurable disease resulting in infant death. Similarly muscular dystrophy is carried by women and afflicts some of the sons of carriers.

■ Psychological well-being. Knowing your family medical history puts you in control of health screening schedules and permits informed decisions.

The underlying concept is that knowledge empowers. It may of course also disturb unnecessarily. Just because your ancestor has had a particular disease it does not mean that you or anyone in your immediate family will develop it. The religious and ethical issues go well beyond the scope of this *How To* guide. Before compiling a family medical history you do need to think about your reaction if you find something unpleasant.

THE NEW FRONTIER

DNA tests are the future of genealogy. This area has the potential to develop into a primary tool for the genealogist, and to yield some of the most exciting finds. In general this potential is not yet quite realised. But it is coming!

Paternity testing, and testing for confirmation of known or suspected relationships within immediate family groups, is well developed. This area of testing is not considered here. There is of course ample scope for family upset and heartache.

What is available for the genealogist is primarily three sorts of testing: deep ancestry, ethnic ancestry, and surname projects. The testing is almost always carried out by a commercial company, and participants need to be aware that the motivation for the companies is not altruism or research for the sake of it but simply to sell their products. There is a tendency for companies to set out the possibility of exciting results which are sometimes but by no means always realised.

DEEP DNA

Deep DNA tests look at the mitochondrial DNA which is passed from mother to children. The mitochondrial DNA we all have comes from our mothers, and from our maternal line. Ultimately the whole of humanity is descended from just a single woman, who lived in Africa somewhere between 50,000 and 200,000 years ago. In genetic terms there really is an Eve. As the human race spread out from Africa mutations occurred to the mitochondrial DNA. As well as being descended from a single Eve, every one of us is descended in the maternal line through one of 36 women representing different groups of humanity. For all 36 women it is possible to suggest where they lived, and indicate at least an approximate time at which each woman lived. The 36 women can be allocated to present-day ethnic groups. For example, the white, Caucasian population is descended from seven women who are believed to have lived in or close to the present European area – women frequently referred to as the 'seven daughters of Eve'.

Benefits of DNA testing?

So what can deep DNA testing tell you? The answer for many people is not actually a lot. In most cases a deep DNA test is little more than a test of ethnicity – and not a particularly good one at that – and most people know their ethnic origin. For someone of European ethnicity the test would show which of the seven European women you are descended from through matrilineal descent, but in many respects this information is redundant. The reality is that when male descent is included all Europeans are descended through many different routes from all seven European women. Of course it is possible that the test would demonstrate that you happen to have a matrilineal ancestor of an ethnicity which surprises you. Some of the more interesting results tend to come from the Americas, where typically matrilineal DNA testing may show that someone who appears to be a white Caucasian of European origin finds they have a matrilineal ancestor who is African or Native American.

Ethnic DNA

An alternative to deep DNA testing is ethnic DNA testing. Typically this utilises markers on the Y-chromosome which is passed from father to son – and which women do not have – though it is possible to utilise also features of the mitochondrial DNA. This is therefore a test which in general only men can have done. It is the hardest and most expensive test to find commercially and is usually carried out as part of a community project.

One such project looks at the peoples who settled the British Isles. Historically the three groups are the Celts, the Anglo-Saxons and the Vikings. Genetic markers indicate that the indigenous population of the British Isles today is about 97% descended from these groups. However, there have been enormous difficulties in distinguishing the Anglo-Saxon and Viking genes, as ethnically these two groups are very close indeed. The best that has been possible is to identify features which belong to one sub-group of Vikings, the Norwegian Vikings, and distinguish these from a group comprising both Anglo-Saxons and Danish Vikings. DNA testing commercially available can distinguish which of the 'three tribes' an individual is descended from through patrilineal descent:

1. Celts

2. Anglo-Saxons and Danish Vikings

3. Norwegian Vikings.

This information maps reasonably well onto a map of the British Isles. Those whose descent is Celtic are likely to find that their recent ancestry is from Ireland, Wales, Western Scotland, the Isle of Man or Cornwall. Those with Norwegian Viking DNA are likely to have recent ancestors from Northern England, Scotland or the area around Dublin, and may well come from one of the Norwegian Viking heartlands, for example Orkney and Shetland. Least informative is DNA from the Anglo-Saxon and Danish Viking group, which has penetrated to all parts of the British Isles.

A test that seems not to exist commercially is one which answers the question 'What is my ethnicity?'. Rather the question seems to have to be posed in the form 'Is my ethnicity X group?'. Within the British Isles a test will look for the three groups above, and in around 3% of cases report simply that the ethnicity is not one of these groups.

Results of ethnic DNA testing

Ethnic DNA testing says more about a people than an individual. There are some stunning results. For example, one of the most dramatic examples of national DNA testing is Iceland. Historically, Iceland was settled by Norwegian Vikings a thousand years ago. People in Iceland consider themselves to be the last Viking nation, the descendants of Viking heroes. In the terms of a popular expression they are 'more Norse than Thor'. Yet the DNA results give a different picture. The mitochondrial results show that the original women settlers of Iceland were around 70% Irish and just 30% Norse. The Y-chromosome results are very different – around 90% Norse and 10% Irish. Quite how this pattern came into being is a matter for the historians. For Icelanders as a people this result is fascinating. Most Icelandic male settlers came from Norway while more than two-thirds of the women came from Ireland.

SURNAME STUDIES

For the genealogist the most exciting area is with the development of surname projects. The concept is that if a very large number of men have markers on their Y-chromosome analysed, then a database can compare results and look for common ancestors within the last thousand years or so. The theory is sound. The problem is that so far not so very many people have had their Y-chromosome analysed, and the databases available are not so very large. Notwithstanding there are some interesting projects.

In theory many of the people who share the same Y-chromosome markers should share the same surname. In a perfect scenario the surname would be one of the earliest to have arisen, would have been created just once, would correspond with a mutation on the Y-chromosome which took place around the time that the surname was created, and the surname would have descended for perhaps 20 generations alongside the biological descent – that is there would be no illegitimacy anywhere.

In practice, these conditions are unusual. In the first place most surnames came into existence separately several times, and may not correspond with an identifiable Y-chromosome mutation. In recent years paternity testing has demonstrated that many children do not have the biological father they think they have, and we have to accept that in any age fathers may not be who we think they are – a big caveat for the genealogist.

Success stories

What is perhaps surprising is the success stories. Two serve to illustrate.

One relates to the surname Macleod. This is the name of a Scottish family which came to prominence in the late middle ages, and which through the clan system was a force to be reckoned with in the Western Isles, Inner Hebrides and West Coast of Scotland. The historic records suggest that every Macleod is descended from an original Leod through his two sons. Y-chromosome testing suggests that around 60% of people bearing the surname Macleod are indeed related to one another in this manner. The remaining 40% presumably reflect adoption of a mother's surname (instead of the father's), adoption of the surname as a mark of allegiance to a leading family, or illegitimacy.

Another relates to the descendants of Genghis Khan. The thirteenth century war-lord who conquered most of Asia is recorded as being exceptionally promiscuous, and consequently as having a very large number of children. As his sons were frequently accorded high status they tended to themselves have large numbers of children. It is believed that characteristics of Genghis Khan's DNA have been identified, allowing for the identification of male descendants of Genghis Khan. About 13% of Asians are believed to be descended in the male line from this one man – something like 300 million people. Adding in descent through female lines it appears that virtually all Asians carry the genes of Genghis Khan who is therefore one of their ancestors. Very many Europeans will also carry the genes of Genghis Khan.

WARNING

STOP! Think before you jump. DNA testing has the potential to produce results that you will not like. Remember that if more than one member of your family take such a test you may in effect be carrying out a paternity test, with the potential for shocking results.

ACTIVITY

Testing services

There are plenty of DNA testing services, easily found through Google ('dna' plus 'genealogy' works well). Investigate what is out there and what would suit you. A very basic DNA check will find out little – you probably need more than the basic packages.

The practicalities are that the companies send you a sterile cheek swab which you use and return to them in the post.

DNA STUDIES

Paternal studies are based on the Y-chromosome which is passed from father to son, almost always without change. Men should

have an identical Y-chromosome to their father, paternal grandfather, brothers, paternal uncles, and indeed all male relatives to
whom they are related through the male line, including very
distant relatives. Once in a blue moon changes in the Y-
chromosome do occur, which are than passed on to male
descendants, and it is these rare changes which make particular
Y-chromosomes specific to a group of male relatives. Any male
can have their Y-chromosome genetic profile tested. Women do
not carry a Y-chromosome, so a sample has to come from a male
relative, say a brother or father.

Testing DNA

Tests typically look at 33 or 46 distinct markers within the Y-
chromosome (the more examined the more accurate the test), and
can be used to establish kinship with other males. Typically a
difference of just two or three markers would indicate that two
individuals are related in the male line, while a match on all 46
markers would indicate common ancestry within at most an
estimated ten generations (that is around 300 to 350 years, which
is within the range of conventional family tree tracing).

DNA Y-chromosome studies enable links to be made with relatives
even when the actually connecting line cannot be traced. As Y-
chromosomes are inherited in the same way as surnames it might
be that all bearers of the same Y-chromosome will also bear the
same surname. In fact it appears that a good proportion of men
with matching Y-chromosomes (that is with only two or three
different markers) bear the same surname (or a spelling variant of
the same surname) – in the region of two-thirds in the British
Isles. This does indicate a remarkably high rate of paternal
parentage being just as people think it is.

There is little point in doing a Y-chromosome DNA test unless you have something with which to compare it, which means you need as big a database as possible. A number of databases do exist. The most promising is that on Ancestry.com – http://www.dna.ancestry.com

Ancestry will give the regions in which bearers of the name Y-chromosome are now living. They will also give names and enable contacts to be made, save where people have chosen to be anonymous. Costs are modest, and the mechanism by which a DNA sample is provided is through a cheek swab. This does of course limit donors to living people – there doesn't yet seem to be a readily available service utilising ancestral hair samples – presumably this will ultimately come.

Also available for men is testing of paternal ancient (ethnic) ancestry, while for both men and women testing of maternal ancient ancestry is offered. Such information is of little genealogical value, but may be of interest nonetheless. The add-on cost is usually small if you are having a Y-chromosome test done.

DNA testing results become more interesting the more people take part. You do really need your ancestry to be online through Ancestry.com or similar to make best use of this exciting new possibility.

All sorts of caveats and warnings go with DNA records online. Check that you are happy with the security of any site to which you give your DNA. There have been all sorts of worries about potential abuse of data (though I'm not aware of any actual cases). Be aware that you are in effect carrying out a paternity test – so if, for example, two brothers each independently used this service, there is the possibility that they could find they in fact had different fathers.

18

Working with Names

A key piece of information you have about ancestors is their name. Both surnames and first names can be rich sources of information.

Sources of British surnames

In the British Isles and throughout Europe, all surnames come from just four sources. These are:

- Patronymics. A surname which says someone is the son of a man identified by his first name. This category includes just about all surnames which end in –son or –s, so surnames like Johnson or Davis for the son of John and the son of David. Sometimes the first name is not immediately recognisable. Bates, for example, is son of Bartholomew. The Celtic languages have given patronymics in Mc- and Mac-, so McAdam or MacDonald. Such forms are particularly common in Scotland and Ireland. Also from Celtic is the prefix O-, as in O'Neill, a form characteristic of Ireland. There is a special class of Welsh surnames in ap-, for example Bevan which is ap-Evan, son of Evan. In the British Isles female forms are not usually found, though they exist elsewhere in Europe – for example, the Icelandic name Jonsdottir means daughter of John.

- Occupational names, as for example Smith or Clerk. Some are not quite as obvious – for example, White is from white-smith, a silver worker. Others relate to occupations that are rarely found today – Cooper, for example, from the occupation cooper, a maker of barrels.

■ Location names which indicate where someone comes from. These can be place names, as Moffat or Durham, or generic descriptions of a place, as Green, Cliff, Meadow. People tend to be given location names when they move away from that place, so a surname such as Moffat probably means that a distant ancestor moved away from the town of Moffat and settled somewhere else, and your link with Moffat is therefore very distant.

■ Nicknames, as Grosvenor (the fat hunter) or Palmer (pilgrim). These are the least common of the four types of surnames.

History of surnames

Surnames have been around for a long time. In most of Europe they were created towards the end of the Middle Ages, and had become firmly established by the sixteenth century. Beware the multiplicity of internet sites which seek to trace surnames back to the Anglo-Saxons or the Vikings – surnames are simply not this old. A very few British surnames may go back to the late twelfth century, and a tiny handful (mostly from Scotland) might possibly go back to the time of William the Conqueror (and were subsequently taken from England to Scotland). For practical purposes, early surnames in the British Isles date from the thirteenth to sixteenth centuries.

Not all surnames are this old. It is common to find late-created surnames, and it may well be that these are in fact the most common surname type. A large group of late-created surnames are those belonging to Jewish people in Central Europe, many of whom were without surnames well into the nineteenth century, but then adopted them as a convenience when living in societies which used surnames. Similarly, Gypsy families have adopted surnames purely as a convenience for living among a non-Gypsy community, and surnames may both be recent creations and vary within a family (so that people who would ordinarily be expected to have the same surname because of their relationship, in fact use different ones). Deliberate changes of name seem reasonably common though often hard to document – for example, a man by the surname of Jones who decides to change it to Taylor for no reason that a genealogist is ever likely to be able to track down.

Many surnames are not old in the form in which they appear. In Britain, the Victorian age saw conscious socially-motivated modification of surnames (for example, Smith to Smyth). Double-barrelled names are rare before the Victorian age, but became relatively common, with the mother's maiden name used as the first of the two joined surnames. This is particularly commonplace when the original surname is common (the obvious example is of course Smith) and may result in subsequent generations dropping the second part of the double name, effectively changing the family surname. Spelling changes are commonplace until recent times – for example, Lemman becomes Lemon – while alternation of spelling within one family can often be found – for example, Rairdon and Reardon. Foreign surnames were frequently assimilated either through translation or a simple Anglicisation of sound and spelling (so Hertz becomes Hart or Harris) or were simply replaced by a name chosen seemingly at random. Archaic forms were also particularly popular in the

Victorian age. For example, Featherstonehaugh as a spelling for Fanshaw.

CHANGING YOUR SURNAME

There is no particular legal impediment to changing your surname. In theory, it should be registered through a simple legal process, but in less bureaucratic ages people simply changed their name by telling people their name was the new form.

While in general surnames pass from father to son, there are numerous exceptions:

■ Illegitimacy. One curious category is the tendency for aristocratic families to use the prefix Fitz- for an acknowledged illegitimate child, so Fitz-Herbert is a surname for the illegitimate son of someone called Herbert.

■ Adoption, where the name of the adopted father is often substituted.

■ Remarriage of the mother changes her surname, and often children by the first marriage start to use the surname of their step father.

■ Through erosion of a double-barrelled surname. From the seventeenth century onwards, it was reasonably common to give a child the mother's maiden name as the first part of a double-barrelled name. Such long surnames were frequently shortened to either the father or mother's name alone.

■ As a requirement for inheriting an estate, where a benefactor may require a beneficiary to adopt his or her surname.

■ Particularly within the Scottish clan system, a surname may be changed to reflect allegiance of a sept – a minor family – to a dominant family, one of the leading clans.

Surnames can be spelt in various different ways. This may reflect limited literacy or illiteracy by bearers of the name, or simply a lack of concern about the spelling – thus William Shakespeare spelt his own surname in three different ways though we can hardly doubt his literacy. To an extent concern over the spelling of one's name is a modern phenomenon. In an age of indexing and official forms, we have all found that wrong spellings cause problems and are therefore alert to them, but a previous age had fewer concerns. Spellings can be changed for social exclusivity – Palmer to Pelmar – or to avoid an unpleasant surname – thus Raper (which in fact has the innocent origin of rope-maker) changes to Roper.

SURNAME PROFILING

Notwithstanding, it is likely that your ancestor bore a surname which was some centuries old. Using surname profiling resources on the internet it is possible to find out something about a surname.

■ What does the surname mean? For almost all names it is possible to say what they mean, and this in theory gives some information about a very distant male-line ancestor. National Trust Names gives brief but accurate information, and is recommended. Beware the many commercial sites and organisations that make a charge for a document which claims to tell you more. What they are advancing is conjecture and wishful thinking.

■ Where does the surname come from? Some surnames have a precise regional point of origin, perhaps even as specific as a county or a part of a county. It is very likely that as recently as the nineteenth century your ancestors were living in the area set out by the surname profiler.

■ What is the social class of a surname? The research around this topic has a sound statistical basis. In theory, it is possible even in twenty-first century Britain to estimate someone's social class from their surname alone. I am inclined to think that this just doesn't work outside of the UK, for example in the US where there has been much more social mobility, but shockingly the statistics indicate that it works within the UK.

■ Is the surname from a process of monogenesis or polygenesis? Big words! Monogenesis means that there was one original bearer of the name. You can spot such surnames if in 1881 there was a very tight regional location. An example is the surname Curnow, which shows up only in the far west of Cornwall. This name is almost certainly from one family founder, and the few Curnows even in western Cornwall suggests that the common ancestor may be as recent as the mid-eighteenth or even early-nineteenth century, so all Curnows today are reasonably closely related. By contrast, polygenesis means there were many founders. There were lots of men who were called Jones because their father was John, lots of smiths called Smith. Most surnames arose more than once and are therefore examples of polygenesis.

■ Using surnames to estimate probability of kinship is not an exact discipline – at least not yet. Some estimates are possible however – see below.

Estimating kinship

Surname-based DNA studies are beginning to produce information about the chance of two people bearing the same surname being related. So far the data lacks quantitative rigour, but some broad guidelines can be established.

▶ Is your surname rare? Surnames like Curnow or Wickenden or Erridge. Is it a form you rarely or never see outside of your known relatives? There is a probability better than 50% that you are related to other people who bear that name in a manner that can be traced. Indeed it may well be that a tree could be drawn up linking together everyone who bears a name such as this.

▶ Is your surname reasonably unusual? Surnames like Everson or Baird or Morley or Palmer. The probability of you being related to all others who bear this name is in the region of 50%.

▶ Is your surname rather more common? Surnames like Harris or Lee or White? There is still a measurable probability of relationship, though the chance is likely to be less than one in four.

▶ Is your surname very common, for example, Smith or Jones? Alas there is unlikely to be a traceable link between you and most other bearers of that name.

CLANS

A special area related to surnames is that of Scottish clans. The clan system is the extended family system which operated in the Scottish Highland and Islands until the late eighteenth century. As a result of mass emigration the descendants of the clans can be found in every corner of the English-speaking world.

A clan was a leading family with its supporters and retainers – who frequently took the surname of the leading family even without a blood link. The old clan system was more or less destroyed by social and political changes in eighteenth century Scotland, and the modern clan system is largely a Victorian revival, assisted by a second revival in the last half of the twentieth century. The concept of a clan is inclusive, that of an extended family. Thus all members of a clan and all descendants (through both male and female lines) may reasonably regard themselves as entitled to wear the appropriate tartan. Clan badges are a different matter – these may well be heraldic devices belonging only to the clan chief.

FIRST NAMES

First names are sometimes informative for the genealogist.

The majority of names within the Western tradition originate in the Bible. John, Mary, David and Ruth are a few of the hundreds of well-established Bible names. A few first names are associated with a particular religious group. The Protestant tradition has tended to use the whole range of Bible names, leading to some noteworthy forms. Aquila, a New Testament name, is found mainly among Quaker and Puritan families. The Roman Catholic tradition draws from an extensive range of saints' names. Damian is a traditional Roman Catholic name and even today unlikely to be found outside of a Roman Catholic family. The Jewish tradition has favoured Old Testament names. Many Jewish families avoid naming children after relatives, so the tendency is to use a great variety of names within a family.

All ages have promoted the names of celebrities. Today it is the names of media figures, pop-stars and sports heroes that influence the names given to babies. In the last few decades the name Harry – once fast declining – has undergone a revival influenced first by

Prince Harry and more recently by Harry Potter, so a name that was becoming dated and unpopular (and arguably was a nickname of Henry rather than a name in its own right) has become a very popular name. In the Victorian age name popularity was most likely to reflect the name of a national hero or be a mark of respect to a royal family. Combinations of names can be informative. Thus Alice Maud Mary is the name of one of Queen Victoria's daughters, and use of these three names in combination implies a reference to this princess.

There are numerous look-up services for first names, many aimed at parents seeking a name for their baby. One important caveat – many of the sites and books about first names put forward absolute rubbish as if it is fact. The emphasis throughout in such lists is on saying nice or at least innocuous things about names. The reality of course is that origins are often not nice, at least to modern sensibilities.

ACTIVITY

Working with surnames
There is one site that stands above all others. At the moment it is primarily for surnames which have their origins in the British Isles, but it is growing fast.

Visit surname profiler: http://www.nationaltrustnames.org

This is a recent research project based at University College London, now supported by the National Trust, which has investigated the distribution of surnames in Great Britain, both current and historic, in order to understand patterns of regional economic development, population movement and cultural identity. For genealogical purposes, it is the records based on 1881 that are of greatest interest – before the twentieth century mobility of families confused the picture.

ACTIVITY

Do you belong to a clan?

▶ If your ancestors are from the Highland and Western Islands of Scotland, then yes you do. Some other parts of Scotland also used tartan, for example, the north-east, as did most Scottish regiments. The tartan will be listed on commercial sites, for example:

http://www.house-of-tartan.scotland.net/house/tfinder.htm/

▶ If your ancestors are from elsewhere in Scotland or Ireland, then the true answer is no. But hundreds of suppliers of tartan clothing (including the one above) will insist that you do in fact have a clan.

▶ If you have any Scottish ancestry whatsoever a special Royal Dispensation entitles you to wear the Royal Family's own tartan, Royal Stewart.

ACTIVITY

Working with first names

http://www.behindthename.com/
This gives a basic etymology and suggests a location for the name. It is a high quality site.

http://www.babynamesworld.com/
A very large site with 11,000+ names.

http://www.askoxford.com/dictionaries/name_dict/?view=uk
This site is the online version of an Oxford dictionary of names with around 6,000 entries. It is now out of date and many of the etymologies are doubtful – but used with caution, it has some interesting material.

19

Recording Your Family Tree

A fun part of having traced your family tree is finding a way to record it. For you this represents a record of achievement, with your findings distilled in a tidy form. And of course all your relatives will want to see a nice, tidy family tree. This is essentially an offline activity, though appropriate charts and software for drawing charts are available online.

CHARTS

Records of families do not easily fit a sheet of paper. Indeed you will soon discover that recording on paper is one of the least satisfactory methods. Basically you either stick to the bare presentation of one line, or you accept an enormously large and unwieldy document with relations tied together with long lines. If you are planning a family gathering and want a wall-sized family tree, then a traditional chart will work. Otherwise it is problematic.

A multiplicity of conventions and chart formats do exist, all with different weaknesses. Be clear before you start of the purpose of the family tree you are drawing. Major types are:

1. Charts that show all direct ancestors of one person (ie which show parents, grandparents, great-grandparents). These do

not show brothers and sisters of ancestors – the piece of paper would become too cluttered. This is the simplest and clearest single page chart, but even here there are problems of too much space for recent ancestors and too little space for distant ancestors.

2. Charts that show selected direct ancestors and their brothers and sisters, typically a family tree of one surname. Using this system you can cover the whole of one line of your family tree on several pieces of paper, or perhaps on many pieces of paper.

3. Charts that show all known descendants of a particular ancestor. This is not for the faint hearted! I have an ancestor born in 1801. With his wife, born 1806, he had 18 children. Twelve of these married and themselves had families, mostly well into double digits, as did their children. My estimate is that there are upwards of 2,000 descendants alive today.

4. Some mix of the above types – however, it is very hard to make this look tidy. It is most likely to work if you want to show how two people are related.

Books

There is a long tradition of publishing books of family history. This is a way of putting together all your research along with charts, photographs, perhaps some historical background as well. Even in the internet age, there is still something very special about a book recording your family tree, as a physical record for future generations. Print on demand publishing services mean that it is now possible to produce very small numbers of a book, even a single copy, and this means that writing a book of your family tree is practical from a cost point of view.

ACTIVITY
_____

Charts

Instant charts:

http://byubroadcasting.org/Ancestors/charts/
http://www.ellisisland.org/genealogy/genealogy_charts.asp

Good range of commercial charts, plus some free materials:
http://www.misbach.org/

Create your own charts with bespoke software:
http://www.smartdraw.com/specials/genealogy.asp

ACTIVITY
_____

Books

No commercial publisher will consider such a book. But there are plenty of 'contribution' or 'subsidy' presses which will produce your book for you. Either you pay all the costs, or the publisher is able to discount a part of these costs because they believe there will be a trickle of sales. If your family is rooted in one location then it is this location that may be the selling point, as it intersects the local history interest market. Writing a narrative and adding photographs and documentation is a time consuming process (as a rule of thumb assume at least three hours per page) but may be something that you want to do and are willing to spend time on.

If you buy a British ISBN number for your book, a copy will be lodged in the British Library ensuring that the book is catalogued and preserved and available to future generations. ISBN numbers used to be free, then available at a peppercorn price, and are now sold only in batches of a minimum of ten. The easiest solution for most self-publishers is to work with a print-on-demand service such as Lulu that will organise an ISBN number and the required lodging of a copy with the British Library.

Two publishers to consider:

▶ For a publisher that may give you some support and help with marketing a family tree book with a strong local history interest, try Dorrance Publishing Company at: http://www.dorrancepublishing.com

▶ The new model for the internet age is 'print on demand', which is much cheaper, but gives you very little support. The major player in this new market is Lulu, at: http://www.lulu.com

ACTIVITY

Posting your family tree to the World Wide Web
Probably this is the sort of publication that you should aim for. It is the most flexible (you can continually add to it) and the most useful for other researchers as there is easy access (in contrast to a low circulation book).

A warning at the outset: be aware of privacy issues. You are making available to the world information which people may consider private. Even information which is publicly available can gain a new significance when assembled on your online family tree. Some sites will not post recent records (typically post-1930), but arguably even this date is a little too recent. Most sites have reasonably robust systems in place to prevent posting of unsuitable material. But the best safeguard is you – think before you post!

Some big sites are:
http://www.ancestry.com
http://www.onegreatfamily.com
http://www.genesreunited.com

What you can expect
You can reasonably expect to make contact with relatives, and to find

out something more about your family. You can expect to understand your own family better through the process of preparing information for upload.

How long will it take?

It is possible to upload the outline of a tree within say an evening's work. If you have a large tree and lots of supporting information you may find that you are looking at very many hours of work, perhaps hundreds of hours. The project is likely to grow through the years. If you maintain a site with new information it is a significant, on-going time commitment, so it is worth while getting right at the outset just how you are planning to upload your tree.

20

Online Recording Options

Broadly you have three choices for an internet family tree.

- Ancestry.com

- Genesreunited.com

- Your own bespoke website

Yes there are other specialist sites – but ancestry.com and genesreunited.com are (arguably) the biggest and best in their slightly different sectors. While other sites are considered below, you will probably want to use one (or more) of the three options above. Just as with online auction sites, you always have a choice, but unless you have a special reason you will end up using the biggest, eBay, because you benefit from everyone else using it.

ACTIVITY

Data control
You need to think about how you feel about family data. How relaxed do you feel about your data? Once it is out there on the net you cannot call it in. The genie is out of the bottle.

▶ Are you content for everything you upload to be available to everyone, for ever?

▶ Do you want to be able to restrict access or even delete the lot?

▶ Do you accept that the nature of the internet is that once something is posted it is out there, but nonetheless want to be able to maintain some degree of control?

If you are happy about general availability to everyone, for ever, that's great. If you want control and privacy you will certainly find systems that appear to offer it, but be aware that on the internet security can be compromised, and frameworks for storing data do change.

OPTION 1 – ANCESTRY.COM

This site is the premier online genealogical resource. (See Figures 11 and 12.) It contains the largest range of worldwide genealogical materials, and the largest number of user-submitted family trees. In addition, it offers very many site-specific features, including its *One-World Tree*, which seeks to link the genealogy of the world. At present hundreds of millions of people are covered by the records held.

Ancestry.com is by no means unique, but it is the biggest and probably the best, and you would have to have a very good reason for uploading to another site.

Note that there are slight national variants of Ancestry. UK genealogists will want to post to: http://www.ancestry.co.uk – though all records are accessible internationally, and the entry page Ancestry.com links to all other Ancestry sites.

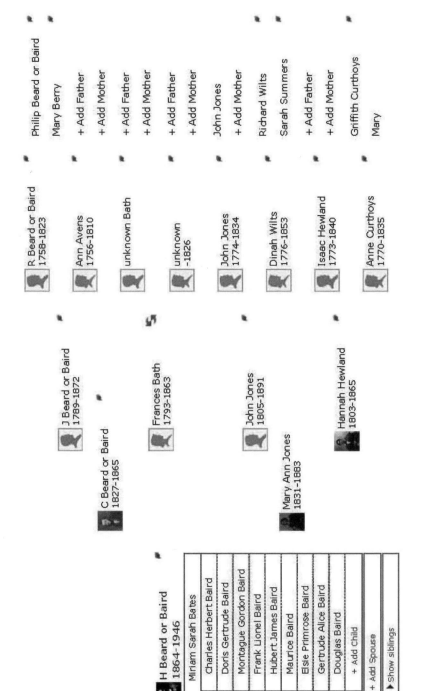

Fig. 11. A family tree on Ancestry.com

Fig. 12. An individual's record on Ancestry.com

ACTIVITY

Know your goals

Know what your goals are. An evening's work is effectively a minimum time to put into uploading your family tree to the internet. Probably you will be devoting a lot more time.

How important to you are the following goals:

▶ Preserving your family tree for the future.

▶ Making your family tree accessible to relatives you know.

▶ Finding more information about your family.

▶ Tracing relatives you do not know, or have lost contact with.

▶ Pursuing a specific end, for example, a one-name study, or a regional study, or a study of an inherited medical condition, or a celebration of a life.

The first three goals are best served by Ancestry.com – the fourth by GenesReunited.com and the final by your own, bespoke site.

ACTIVITY

Share your family tree

Do you want to share your family tree with the following people:

▶ Your immediate family.

▶ Your more distant relatives.

▶ People you are related to but do not know.

▶ Local historians, social historians, or anyone who may have an interest.

▶ The world.

▶ Posterity – your descendants and relatives perhaps yet unborn.

Your answers influence the sort of online family tree you should consider. If you are keen on the widest possible general dissemination of your family tree then Ancestry.com is unbeatable. If you specifically want to track down relatives then the key site is GenesReunited.com

OPTION 2 – GENESREUNITED.COM

GenesReunited offers a different emphasis to Ancestry.com. Based on the sort of databases which created FriendsReunited, the social website reuniting lost friends, GenesReunited has as its primary goal reuniting relatives. Both Genes- and Friends-Reunited are run by the same company, and the feel of searching their database is very similar.

The function of searching for lost relatives is not unique to GenesReunited – you can indeed do this through Ancestry – but it is the special strength of GenesReunited. By posting to GenesReunited you are in effect specifically advertising that you want relatives to get in touch with you. And they will! With a tree that is anything but the smallest, you can more or less guarantee contact from relatives, and you will therefore discover cousins you did not know existed.

The downside of GenesReunited is the tendency of people to send a contact message without thinking whether there is any real chance of a relationship. You will inevitably get emails that run to the following form:

> 'Hi! I see you have an ancestor called John Jones. So have I. Mine lived in a different part of the country and was born ten years later, but do you think we could be related?'

Rarely a week goes by without me receiving an email in this form. I regard it as a form of spam – but if I want the real links GenesReunited can offer, I have to put up with it.

OPTION 3 – YOUR OWN WEBSITE

There are some special reasons for establishing your own website, and these are looked at below. A personal genealogy website does not of course have to be your only website, and may well be supported by listings on Ancestry and GenesReunited.

MORE ABOUT ANCESTRY.COM

This website is part of a very large business, The Generations Network http://www.tgn.com. This organisation operates from Provo, Utah in the US – from a part of the world where genealogy is big business. Though not directly linked with the Jesus Christ Church of Latter Day Saints (Mormons) in Utah, The Generations Network benefits from the pool of genealogically skilled labour in the region.

When using Ancestry.com you need to be aware that you are dealing with a big business – one with revenue of $150 million per year and employing 1,300 people (2009 figures). They are completely different from the amateur-run websites in genealogy where you may well find the people running the website are really interested in your personal research. Rather Ancestry.com are a for-profit, private company, the biggest genealogy company in the world. No one there is likely to be interested in giving you free advice, though they may be interested in customer feedback on the web interface, and interested to learn of customer problems with a view to improving their search system.

When you upload your family tree to Ancestry.com you are in effect giving them for free materials which they can and will sell. Because it is good for them to have your material, Ancestry.com make no charge to upload family trees. Their motive is profit not altruism, but you benefit because you get access to the best available repository for free.

The same company runs FamilyHistory.com – so records you post to Ancestry.com will find there way to this site also. They also publish *Ancestry Magazine*.

So what's on Ancestry.com?

There are over five billion records, which are growing rapidly, on this site. Coverage is good for the UK, Australia, the US and Canada, fair for many continental European countries (particularly Germany), and patchy elsewhere. Most of these records can only be seen by subscribers, though everyone can see the index. It is through subscription that Ancestry makes their money.

Many records are duplicated, and you need several different records to build the life of an individual, so five billion records does not translate into five billion people. It probably translates into around a billion people. Bear in mind too that Ancestry covers mainly the nineteenth century (when the population of the world was a lot smaller than its present six billion) and is strongest for Britain, the British Empire and the US. A very high proportion of the people you will be interested in are recorded somewhere on Ancestry.com.

What does Ancestry.com cost?

It is possible to upload your family tree and view it without paying a subscription – in effect using Ancestry.com as a free data store. It is even possible for you to give someone else access to your tree without you or them paying. These are real, useful freebies. You can search their indexes without cost, and the indexes alone provide a lot of useful material. Some records are available for free, including the whole of the British 1881 census.

But in all probability you are going to want to pay a modest subscription to Ancestry.com to search their records – details of prices are on their site.

For many years they have offered a service where you can try for free before you buy. Ancestry.com offer a 14-day free trial. This offer has been in place for a long time, and is likely to continue. If you work fast and do your searches in that 14-day period, you can actually make a lot of progress with your family tree without paying a penny. It's a good offer!

BEWARE! Ancestry.com take your credit card details if you sign up to their 14-day free trial and will automatically take a first subscription after your free trial if you do not contact them to cancel. Automatic taking of first subscription and indeed subsequent automatic renewal of subscriptions is a bit of an issue and has received media attention. If you forget to cancel, then the first you will know is when you see your credit card statement – assuming of course you check your credit card statement thoroughly.

You must use a web link or telephone in order to cancel. The consensus view of users is that cancellation is very easy, so there is some good news. Lots of people really do not like this business practice of automatic renewal, but the choice is put up with it or don't use Ancestry.com, and as there isn't a good alternative most put up with it.

MORE ABOUT GENESREUNITED.COM

GenesReunited is part of the same organisation that created the better known FriendsReunited. The ethos of the site is very different to Ancestry.com in that most of the content of GenesReunited is user submitted.

GenesReunited is a social networking service, and it is important to see it in this light. Friends Reunited boasts about 20,000,000 members in the UK alone – more than half of UK households. GenesReunited is somewhere behind that, but gaining ground fast. FriendsReunited can be joined with just a few minutes time to input, for example, your school, your name and your contact details, and millions of us have done just this. A few add more information, perhaps a photograph or something about their family or work. It is all very quick to do. By its nature a family tree takes rather more work to load onto GenesReunited, and inevitably this is holding back numbers of users.

The basic business model for both FriendsReunited and GenesRe-united is that they charge to put individuals in touch with one another. If you want to get in touch with a friend or relative you have to subscribe so that you can place an email through their system, which uses a double blind system both to ensure the privacy of users and to ensure that you have to pay for the services of GenesReunited. Recently, FriendsReunited has increased the free component, and it may be that GenesReunited will follow.

Without paying a subscription you can browse what is in effect an index on GenesReunited, but if you find someone you want to contact you have no option other than paying. GenesReunited are proactive in trying to put you in touch with relatives, particularly through their idea of trump cards, where card details of your ancestor and that of another contributor will be matched and emailed to both. It can be most exciting!

Without paying a subscription you can upload a tree. By doing this you give GenesReunited content that they can use to persuade other people to sign up. It is possible for someone else to contact you (at no charge to you) and you then switch to email and therefore you do not pay. But in practice you will probably want to see their GenesReunited tree – for which you have to pay.

You can either type your tree straight into GenesReunited, or upload a gedcom file. It is practical to create your tree on Ancestry.com, download a gedcom from this and upload to GenesReunited. Beware – at the moment there seems to be no way to download a tree from GenesReunited, so you cannot go the other way. If your tree is created on GenesReunited, then there it stays.

The UK is the strongest base for GenesReunited, and while others countries will presumably catch up they are not there yet.

One other consideration with GenesReunited is that it is not a particularly pretty site to work with. Rather the format is that of a portal which enters and retrieves data. It works, but other sites look nicer.

OTHER COMPANIES

There is of course much more choice than just Ancestry and GenesReunited.com. Some of the other big players are:

Genealogy at: http://www.genealogy.com operates the World

Family Tree, a site with a similar structure to Ancestry – but smaller. You cannot directly contact someone who has posted a tree – rather the request goes to the site, who pass to the tree poster the information that someone wants to get in touch, for the tree-poster to respond to or otherwise. Correction of errors is cumbersome and slow through this site – indeed the site seems to end up with two 'alternatives', the right and the wrong information, with the latter also preserved for posterity.

Kindred Connections at: http://www.kindredconnections.com and My Trees at: http://www.mytrees.com (the same organisation) have both user submitted information and extracted information, from births, marriages and deaths (BMD) and census records. You pay to access their database. This is nowhere near the size of the big players, but they do have some records the others don't.

Family Search at: http://www.familysearch.org is the Jesus Christ Church of Latter Day Saints (Mormon) database. You will almost certainly use it because it contains by far the largest collection of transcribed and searchable parish register entries, along with a massive quantity of other BMD and census information. It is a superb site to search. You can also use it as a repository for your family information. Family Search encourages GEDCOM submission – which means you need to enter your data into the GEDCOM program which you have on your computer, and upload the file, not the raw data. Records submitted are not immediately available, but are updated some weeks or months later. Like Ancestry, Family Search is based in Utah, though the two are separate. The Mormon religious interest in genealogy is to permit the posthumous baptism of relatives, and you will find many individuals in their records listed as 'cleared', ie posthumously baptised, where a Mormon has established that these individuals are relatives and baptised them. Your views on this practice may be a factor in your decision to use or not use their services. A key difference with the Family Search system is that both uploading and searching pedigrees is free – a marked contrast to the commercial databases. Additionally records which they have which are still not online, for example on microfiche or CD-ROM, are typically available for purchase or loan at cost price.

Rootsweb at: http://www.rootsweb.com is another product from Ancestry.com. The primary difference is in the way they store the data. With Ancestry.com searches are individual-by-individual; with Rootsweb it is more tree-by-tree. Does it make much difference? It is easy to prefer one interface to another, but in terms of the sort of information available and the ease of finding it, the answer has to be no, not really. Rootsweb is free both to upload data and to search, while Ancestry.com charges to see the results of many searches. But Ancestry has a lot more data than Rootsweb.

One Great Family at: http://OneGreatFamily.com automatically merges data from submitted family trees with the intention to create one great family tree. Sounds great, but this is done automatically by computer. The result is links that are just not correct, so that at best everything this site produces would have to be checked, and at worst a lot of mistaken, computer-generated wrong links are cluttering up databases. As a site, I think it needs revising.

AVOIDING RE-ENTRY OF DATA

Typing a family tree of anything but the smallest size into any of the online systems takes a long time – as does entering data into software packages that draw trees. You want to avoid entering data more than once.

Transfer of data is possible through a type of file called GEDCOM. This records in a machine-readable family the names of individuals, the relationships, and life-time events including birth, marriage and death.

Broadly, GEDCOM works. It certainly transfers the mass of data without many problems. But beware:

■ It does not transfer stories, pictures, audio or video files.

■ It should be checked, for example, in family trees which include the marriage of cousins.

Ancestry.com allows both upload and download of GEDCOM files. GenesReunited permits only upload. So if you create your family tree on GenesReunited, you have to retype it to move it somewhere else. Better create on Ancestry.com.

MORE ABOUT YOUR OWN WEBSITE

The most flexible option is of course your own website. Whether you want to go down this road depends on two sorts of considerations:

1. What you want to achieve, and why this is better done on your own website rather than on one of the established sites.

2. How comfortable you are with setting up a website.

The sort of things that may be better on your own website include:

■ A study of everyone who has the same surname (a one-name study).

■ A clan website reuniting members of a Scottish clan, where the fact of bearing a particular surname gives 'membership' to a group.

■ A website around the ancestry, and perhaps descendants too, of one particular person – perhaps a present for grandma's 90th birthday!

■ A study of a location or region and all families in it, rather than a study of one related family. Thus a study of the inhabitants of a particular parish in the eighteenth and nineteenth centuries will include much genealogical data, but fits poorly in conventional sites.

Setting up your own website does require either specific skills or use of packages and systems which do part of the work for you. Options include:

■ HTML – the basics of html, the computer language in which web pages are usually written, are reasonably simple, but a website which uses only the basics will look well, basic. We have all become familiar with highly proficient internet design, and amateurish work looks just that. Not really a skill you learn just to set up one website.

■ WYSIWYG editors – packages such as Dreamweaver and FrontPage which convert a word-processing or similar file into a web page. Very clever, though you do still need to put some time into learning the packages.

ACTIVITY

View examples

▶ For a surname that interests you, search in Google for it and 'one name study'. Very many surnames have been covered by specialists.

▶ Compare with a site that has won lots of awards: http://www.bairdnet.com

Going it alone by setting up your own website is not an easy option, and you do need web-page design skills (or need to be prepared to learn them). Much information on the practicalities of setting up your own genealogy website from scratch can be found at: http://www.cyndislist.com/construc.htm

A very simple solution for your own family tree website is to use a blog as a framework. A blog – otherwise weblog – is a template for a webpage which you adapt as you wish. The biggest supplier is Blogspot at: http://www.blogger.com. This is a quick and easy way to get a webpage up and running. Some very basic familiarity with html might help, but most users learn as they go, so there is a negligible initial learning curve. You can indeed manage much knowing no html at all.

You also need web space. The option exists of buying space, though most users can find free web space given by their internet service provider (ISP), or available online. Blogs usually provide free web space.

A basic personal genealogy website is therefore very cheap or free, and need not take too much time or effort. However, if you want to upload video files (which take a lot of space) or use special features such as online chat rooms, you may find that you need more web space and more technical ability. Even here though the trend is towards tools that are ever more user friendly.

21

Problems of Online Trees

Online family trees are great, but there are some problems, and you need to have your eyes open when you use them. There are some things you might think they jolly well should be able to do (like drawing family trees) and which they cannot do at all well. There some more serious problems lurking too.

ONLINE FAMILY TREES AND DRAWING FAMILY TREES

Online sites are not good ways to draw family trees. Yes, they can do something, but the results are poor. If drawing family trees is what you really want to do, you may well be best using bespoke software or stencils that will let you do this. This will make the best job possible.

The hypertext format of the online sites is ideal for presenting a family tree to people who are familiar with using computers. As more and more of the world fall into this category there is a sense that this is the future. Maybe drawn and printed trees are going the same way as parchment and quills.

GEDCOM PROBLEMS

Lots of problems around using online trees relate to using GEDCOM, so it is as well to know a little about it. GEDCOM stands for GENealogical Data COMmunication, and is the usual method for transferring genealogical data between different applications. Just about all genealogical software uses this format (and if you have software that doesn't, bin it!) In format the file is plain text (usually ASCII) with meta data providing the links.

Most genealogists need to know almost nothing about the technical side of GEDCOM, but there are a few issues to be aware of:

■ This is a remarkably enduring program. The version presently in use – 5.5 – was launched in 1996, and with just minor modifications is still in use. Version 6.0 is in beta stage and not in general use, and seems to be facing lengthy delays (as at March 2009). You can use GEDCOM confident that it will not become obsolete in no time.

■ While GEDCOM is standard, many applications have proprietary versions with various add-ons. Data encapsulated in these add-ons will be lost when you move data between applications.

■ At present GEDCOM does not support any characters not in ASCII, so names using non-standard letters or in different alphabets must be transcribed. Version 6.0 will fix this.

■ GEDCOM copes poorly with name changes (other than through marriage) and does not have a convenient way of entering nicknames.

■ GEDCOM can cope with (for example) marriage of cousins, but it struggles with most data conflicts. For example, adoption really does not fit in the present GEDCOM system as it will not accept that an individual may have both biological and adoptive parents.

- GEDCOM is very traditional in that it expects a couple to marry before children can be entered. It is possible to enter a 'custom event', say an engagement, to circumvent this problem (though even this suggests a degree of formality in the relationship).

- GEDCOM struggles with such things as bigamy, or a man having a family by two different women at the same time.

LIBEL

You are responsible for the content that you put on any website. Be careful that everything you say on a website is true and can be proved to be true, which in the context of genealogy means referencing to records. Be very careful not to say anything about a relative, particularly a living relative, which is both unverified and unpleasant. The ultimate sanction in most legal systems is that you could be prosecuted for libel for posting defamatory comments.

CONFIDENTIAL INFORMATION

Be aware also that information you make available about yourself or others may include your date of birth, place of birth and mother's maiden name – all information that banks and other financial institutions use to verify identity.

22

Finding Living Relatives

One of the most exciting areas of family tree research can be finding living relatives. These might be people you once knew but have lost touch with, or people you know nothing about.

CONTACTING LOST RELATIVES

Sites including GenesReunited and Ancestry.com enable you to get in touch with relatives. You might also be able to locate a relative through FriendsReuited, or through a subscription-based person finding service.

How many cousin contacts you can make or receive depends on factors including the number of ancestors you upload, and the number of generations you have taken your family back. The contacts will vary greatly in terms of the quality of genealogical information they may give.

The most informative contacts are of course the closest ones – first cousins (who share your grand-parents) or second cousins (who share your great-grandparents). You may well find you both have recollections of a particular relative. It is reasonable to expect some contacts at this degree of closeness through the two major online sites. They are the most exciting contacts.

More distant contacts can still be informative. My most distant contact which was informative has been with a fourth cousin, who has a photograph of our great-great-great grandfather, a man born in 1801, and with a fifth cousin, who had a fragment of information I needed.

It has to be said that a lot of distant contacts are of little immediate interest. For distant ancestors most genealogists are working with records of birth, marriage and death, census records, and other established genealogical sources. Unless one or other of the cousins has some personal information handed down, there is little interest in the contact. I have had around a dozen contacts in the last year from distant relatives who share an ancestor with me born in 1700. Not one has been able to add any information. Yes we are related, distantly, but what follows from this? Genealogists are coming to realise that we are all related to everyone anyway.

Site-Moderated Emails

Initial contacts are likely to be through site-moderated emails. This system gives a degree of privacy and safety to both parties.

Be aware however that you are probably not as anonymous as you think! Once you have given basic information about yourself person-finder sites can track you down (complete with address from the electoral register, and possibly a BT telephone number). All of us are increasingly findable even through Google.

Personal Emails

It is convenient to move from site mediated emails to personal emails as soon as possible. You might well find that the email exchange takes off. While most exchanges are just two or three emails, I have discovered one relative who has now sent me close to 200 emails.

MEETING RELATIVES

The obvious follow-up to a contact with a relative is a meeting.

Be aware that just because you share ancestors doesn't mean you actually know this person. Possibly you have some family information about them which might give you some confidence – but in general it is sensible to treat a meeting as you would a complete stranger. A public place is prudent.

23

Genealogical Miscellany

Many of the most satisfying genealogical finds are those that go beyond ordinary written records. There is a large and varied category of miscellaneous sources, many of which are now firmly rooted in the internet.

PHOTOGRAPHS

Some of the most exciting materials which the online sites can offer are photographs.

The earliest practical photography – daguerrotypes – dates from 1839, but you would be very lucky indeed if you found something this early. Photography became more common in the 1850s and 1860s, particularly associated with the ambrotype process, and photographs from this period do turn up. Towards the end of the century new and cheaper processes using photographic plates and later film became available, so that from the last decade of the nineteenth century families of all social classes were having photographs taken, and it is very likely indeed that your ancestors living at this time were photographed.

Most early photographs are of course black and white, occasionally hand coloured by an artist, with colour photography coming into common use as late as the 1950s and 1960s. Formal photographs – for example, wedding photographs – tended to

Fig. 13. A formal family group photograph, 1914, available online.

Fig. 14. A group of friends relevant to eight different family trees, available online.

Fig. 15. A formal wedding group, 1919, with people positioned on bride's and groom's side, available online.

140

Fig. 16. A father and son photograph, about 1899, available online.

be in black and white even after colour became readily available. Often black and white was perceived as being of a higher quality, or simply as more formal and therefore more appropriate to mark a big occasion.

If you are lucky you will have such photographs or know a relative who has them. Alternatively you might see what the internet can do.

The earlier photographs are mainly posed, studio pictures, often of excellent quality, and with a wealth of information contained in the picture. Families have tended to keep them, so it is very likely that if you don't have such photographs one of your cousins somewhere will. Of course it might be necessary to find your cousin first.

Ancestry has a large collection of photographs, and if you are very lucky you might find a photograph of your ancestor with a simple name search on their database. Their collection is already enormous, and it is fast growing.

Photographs include the following:

Portraits
These exist from the 1850s, in theory even earlier, though photography became far more affordable in the 1890s. The first world war gave a special impetus to photographs. It is possible to find quality photographs of ancestors born as early as around 1800, and in theory from earlier. Studio portraits can be among the most satisfying links with an ancestor.

Group photographs
An early wedding group is one of the most exciting photographic

finds because of the great number of people shown – though images of individuals may be less sharp than ideal. It can take a lot of patience to identify most or all people in a group. Many are carefully posed with a bride's side and groom's side, so, for example, parents of each can sometimes be identified simply on the basis of where they are sitting.

Pictures of buildings

The interest associated with such photographs varies greatly. There are a lot of photographs of this nature on Ancestry.com. Most searchers react with disappointment when a picture labelled with an ancestors name turns out to be, for example, a modern photograph of the church in which they were christened. Pictures of buildings contemporary with an ancestor's life can often be found on appropriate local history websites.

Gravestones

Quite a large number of photographs posted on Ancestry.com are of gravestones. If you do post such a picture, take care to record a transcription of the gravestone, and note exactly where it is (particularly important in the case of some of our enormous city cemeteries). Regrettably, a majority of posters seem not to do this, and the majority of photographs of gravestones are largely unreadable snaps without supporting information.

Documents

Absolutely any document can be loaded as a picture to the Ancestry site, so you never know quite what you might find. Certificates of birth, marriage and death and census extracts are common.

Audio and video

There has long been a tradition of taking photographs, both formal and snaps, but not of recording speech. Despite half a century of the ready availability of tape recorders, it is rare to find a recording made of the speech of older members in a family. Uploaded film and video is similarly rare. If you can source a recording of your ancestor this can be uploaded to ancestry.com. If you are very lucky indeed you might even find such a recording.

Photographs

Put lots of effort into finding photographs as they make ancestors real in a way that few other sources can do. Check the following:

▶ What photographs do you have tucked away?

▶ What photographs do relatives have?

▶ Search on Ancestry.com for photographs.

▶ Ask genealogy contacts what photographs they have.

▶ Search local history websites.

The National Portrait Gallery has an enormous collection of images including many photographs, all indexed and with the index available online. Sometimes a picture is available on the website; alternatively it can be obtained at a low cost.

FAMILY STORIES AND ORAL HISTORY

You may find a family story posted to Ancestry.com. Typically such a story might be an anecdote, additional information about occupation or military service, or even a transcript of something the ancestor has written. You may also find that distant cousins have heard the same family story, remembered in two long-separated family branches. This is great confirmation of the story.

Family stories can be exceptionally long-lasting. My own family has preserved a story through an oral tradition for 300 years, and I count as one of the most satisfying pieces of genealogy I have engaged in confirmation that this story is indeed correct. Family stories can also be infuriatingly garbled. Generations are often muddled – something related as happening to someone's grandfather actually happened to their grandfather's grandfather. Relationships can be vague. A cousin may turn out to be a cousin by marriage, and in any case may be more distant than a simple first cousin.

The stories that are most likely to be true are those which describe ancestors in a not wholly favourable light, or which include detail which is strictly irrelevant to the story. It seems very rare for a story about an ancestor to be completely fabricated.

ACTIVITY

Be willing to believe stories
▶ Find out what stories you or your relatives know.
▶ Consider how you might check them out.

SHARING RESEARCH COSTS

Most of the people you contact through an online site will be actively tracing a family line. There are obvious chances for pooling resources. The simplest is of course sharing research already done. However, it is possible to take sharing to a new level by sharing future research costs. This is particularly useful when you need to buy birth, marriage and death certificates, as the cost can add up quickly.

NEWSPAPER CUTTINGS

Most families received some form of coverage in newspapers in the late nineteenth and early twentieth centuries.

The Times newspaper has an old paper index with three volumes per year. However, it is now available in digital format in which it can be searched by text. If your ancestor was mentioned in *The Times* it is now practical to find the reference. The index to *The Times* is in theory available from your computer, but it is a subscription service and the cost is prohibitive. Probably you will prefer to access it through a public library. Records include announcements of births (usually very brief indeed, and in the nineteenth century typically giving simply the name of the father and whether the baby a son or daughter) announcements of engagement and marriage, and obituaries. These are all good genealogical material.

The vast majority of newspapers in Britain, including virtually all local papers, have no indexes (with the possible exception of issues published in very recent years). While access to the newspapers is possible through specialist newspaper libraries and local repositories they are rarely practical for the genealogist to search.

Cuttings tend to be preserved by families. You can reasonably expect to find through contacts with cousins:

■ notices of deaths and funerals, possibly also obituaries;

■ notices of marriage; occasionally (and much more rarely) notices of births, christenings or other milestones;

■ newspaper coverage of family disasters: strange deaths, injuries, criminal activity;

■ newspaper accounts of achievements: academic, military.

ACTIVITY

The Times

▶ Find where you can access *The Times* online.

▶ Spend an hour or two (or more) entering names of relatives, and see what might appear.

PUBLICATIONS

In theory it is possible to track down anything your ancestor might have published through national repositories. In Britain, the theory is that ALL publications are lodged with the British (Museum) Library. Their catalogue is available online. You can certainly type the names of their ancestors into their catalogue and see what might surface.

In fact there are problems. If your ancestor has the name John Jones (as do several of mine), then finding an item is inevitably problematic. Early indexing was imperfect – multi-authored work, for example, is often listed under just the first named author. Not everything someone wrote was actually lodged in the British Library, even though this was the law. Many books were privately published, in effect printed without going through a major press, and are not properly recorded. Music is notoriously difficult to find.

Perhaps the easiest way to find a copy of a publication by an ancestor is to find a relative who has a copy.

Find an ancestor's book

▶ Access the British Library Catalogue at: http://www.bl.uk

▶ Spend an hour or two (or more) entering names of relatives, and see what might appear.

PERSONAL BELONGINGS AND JEWELLERY

Personal belongings have not survived in the quantities we might hope. Our ancestors had less 'stuff' than we probably do, it was typically used until it fell to bits, and often was not of a quality that encouraged preservation. Items that do turn up reasonably frequently include:

- Bibles, prayer books, school prize books. Inscriptions can be informative.

- Embroidery samplers.

- Items related to a trade, for example, a carpenter's apprentice piece.

- Items of jewellery.

- Christening gowns.

- Personal clothing.

Sometimes an item needs interpretation. Take, for example, the text of a Victorian embroidery sampler with genealogical information:

In Early years I this Peace Began,
From thread to thread I travel on,
In Hope to find that distant shore,
Where Angels shine forever more.
SP JP DP HP RP MP HP GP BP SP
Eliza Palmer
Aged 10 years
1843

The spelling 'peace' for 'piece' is original. Here some information is obvious – the name and age of Eliza Palmer. The string of initials all ending in P needs decoding – in fact it is a list of her brothers and sisters. The order is that of their date of birth, and it therefore provides useful information on their order of birth. Potentially the verse should be traceable and may indicate a book available to the family, though in this case I have drawn a blank.

ACTIVITY

Looking at personal possessions
▶ Take a look at any personal possession of an ancestor that you or a relative might have
▶ Think about ways in which you might investigate it for family tree information.

HAIR SAMPLES

Through the Victorian age and well into the twentieth century, the practice of taking hair samples was very common indeed. They were used both as love tokens and as keepsakes of people who had died. Many of them have been preserved. Quite what anyone today ever does today with such samples is a moot point, and I admit a certain squeamishness with such remembrances.

They are of course a most personal link with an ancestor.

It is possible to extract DNA from hair, and this circumstance may one day give a special value to preserved hair. Mitochondrial DNA can be found in the hair itself, but y-DNA requires the root of the hair, and therefore is only possible if the hair has been pulled out (which it sometimes is when it is just a few hairs in a locket given as a love token). Extracting DNA from hair is difficult, time consuming and therefore expensive. You would not choose to be getting your DNA sample in this way. For the genealogist there is no easily accessed path for getting a DNA test on a hair sample, but such will presumably come. Should you have access to a hair sample, keep it for the future!

24

Accent and Dialect

We all know that how someone speaks gives a clue to their place of origin and perhaps more, yet little effort has so far been put into using this as a genealogical tool. Today in the British Isles it is usually possible to identify the region of the country someone is from by how they speak. A century ago accents were distinct at the level of counties, and perhaps at an even more local level. People are often poor at identifying accents, but we do all notice if an accent is different from the one found in our local area. If we spend time with a person from outside our area we note specific words, idioms and speech mannerisms that are different to ours.

ACTIVITY

Collecting information

When you are asking a relative for recollections about an ancestor, ask them also about how that person spoke. All this is potentially useful genealogical information, and frequently overlooked.

▶ Did they have an accent that was different from people around them?

▶ Did they have unusual words for things?

▶ Did they use strange expressions?

▶ Did they have odd ways of saying particular words?

▶ Did they have strange family nicknames for relatives?

ACTIVITY

What does it mean?

You need to find a way of interpreting the information you have gathered.

One sort of starting point is in dialect dictionaries. About the most you can hope for from the internet is access to library catalogues to find out just what is available. Very few dialect dictionaries are online.

▶ The small dialect dictionaries published by Abson Books are easily available, both in libraries and in bookshops. They now cover almost the whole of Britain and Ireland, and are a good starting point. If your ancestor *picked the washing from the line*, then this series of dictionaries will tell you this is a West Country expression.

▶ Most English and Welsh counties are covered by a late Victorian dictionary published by the English Dialect Society. Some have been revised and are available in modern editions. Be aware that a word found in a dictionary for one county may not be unique to that county.

▶ Scotland is particularly well served by dialect dictionaries. The *Concise Scots Dictionary* is the usual starting point.

Take particular note of how your ancestor addressed relatives. If grandmother was called *Bobby*, it might suggest *bubbe*, the Yiddish word for grandmother. Anyone else in a family called by something like this might be *bubbeleh*, the British Yiddish for *darling*, while *tante* (pronounced *ton-tay*) is *aunt*. Such words are evidence of Jewish ancestry, perhaps unsuspected. You may possibly find traces of Welsh, Gaelic and Romany words in your ancestors' language.

25

Final

I hope that by the time you get to the end of this *How To* book you will know a lot more about your family than you did before you started. I hope you have enjoyed the journey.

You will never reach the end of your genealogical research. Indeed the future for genealogy is a network of interlinked genealogies available online, showing the relationship of each one of us to more and more people world-wide. The research is being done by thousands of enthusiasts, most amateur, and the results are beyond the dreams of genealogists in the pre-internet age. Every newly available archive contributes, as does every single piece of information submitted by individuals. Future generations will have an extraordinary wealth of material available.

For our generation is the fun of the search. Good luck in all your research!

Key Websites

NAME SITES

http://www.nationaltrustnames.org.uk (surnames)

http://www.house-of-tartan.scotland.net/house/tfinder.htm (Scottish surnames)

http://www.behindthename.com/ (surnames)

http://www.babynamesworld.com (first names)

http://www.askoxford.com/dictionaries/name_dict (first names)

SOURCES FOR BIRTHS, MARRIAGES AND DEATHS

http://www.bmdindex.co.uk (England and Wales, post-1837)

www.scotlandspeople.gov.uk (Scotland, post-1855)

http://www.eneclann.ie (Ireland)

http://www.familysearch.org (World, mainly pre-1860)

http://www.vitalrec.com (post-1837)

CENSUS SITES

http://www.nationalarchives.gov.uk/census (links to all UK censuses)

http://www.censusuk.co.uk (UK census portal)

http://www.1911census.co.uk (1911 census England, Wales and Scotland)

http://www.familyrecords.gov.uk (1841 to 1901 censuses)

http://www.scotlandspeople.gov.uk (for Scotland)
http:/www.census-online.com/links (US and Canada)
http://www.coraweb.com.au/census.htm (Australia)

Pedigree sites

www.ancestry.com (Ancestry website)
http://www.ancestry.co.uk (UK portal of Ancestry)
http://www.genesreunited.com (contacting relatives)
http://www.1837online.com (major pedigree site)
http://www.onegreatfamily.com (major pedigree site; part of Ancestry)
http://www.rootsweb.com (major pedigree site)
http://www.genealogy.com (operates the World Family Tree)
http://www.kindredconnections.com (major pedigree site)
http://www.mytrees.com (major pedigree site)
http://www.familysearch.org (major pedigree site)

National variants of Ancestry.com

http://www.ancestry.co.uk (UK and Ireland)
http://www.ancestry.ca (Canada including 1911 Canadian Census)
http://www.ancestry.com.au (Australia plus the UK and Ireland)
http://www.ancestry.de (Germany)
http://www.ancestry.co.it (Italy)
http://www.ancestry.com (US and World)

Heraldry

http://www.college-of-arms.gov.uk (College of Arms)
http://www.lyon-court.com (Court of the Lord Lyon – Scotland)

Extensive list of genealogy links

http://www.cyndislist.com (enormous list)

Look-ups

http://www.ukgenealogy.co.uk/lookup.htm (UK look-ups)
http://www.cyndislist.com/lookups.htm (worldwide look-ups)

Directories

http://www.galegroup.com (UK)
http://www.uscitydirectories.com (US)
http://www.tpl.toronto.on.ca/localhistory/directories1.html
    (Canada)

Charts

http://byubroadcasting.org/Ancestors/charts (free charts)
http://www.ellisisland.org/genealogy/genealogy_charts.asp (free
    charts)
http://www.misbach.org (charts to buy and for free)
http://www.smartdraw.com/specials/genealogy.asp (software to
    draw charts)

Some other great sites

http://www.cwgc.org/ (Commonwealth War Graves Commission)
http://www.bbc.co.uk/history/war/wwone (BBC First World War)
http://www.familyrecords.gov.uk/topics/wills.htm (wills)
http://www.movinghere.org.uk (migration to Britain)
http://www.ellisisland.org/ (migration to USA)
http://en.wikipedia.org/wiki/Poor_Law (understanding the Poor Law)

http://www.old-maps.co.uk/ (UK historic maps)

http://www.dna.ancestry.com (major DNA site)

http://www.friendsreunited.com/ (good for contacting living relatives)

Index

accent, 151–152

adoption, 101, 132

Africa, 92

agricultural labourer, 38, 61

Alice Maud Mary, 107

ambrotype, 137

Ancestry.com, 115, 120–121, 134, 142–143

Anglo–Saxon, 79, 92

Aquila, 106

archival records, 14

aristocracy, 65

Asia, 95–96

audio clips, 144

Australia, 24, 36, 56, 121

Baird, 105

baker, 61

banns, 19

baronet, 69–70

barracks, 41

Bates, 7, 12

Bible, 148

Bible names, 106

bigamy, 133

birth certificates, 19–22

birth records, 18

bishops' transcripts, 20

blog, 129

blue blood, 66

BMD, 18, 23–26, 125

boarding school, 75

books, 110–111, 147

British Library, 111, 147

burials, 19–20

butcher, 61

Canada, 24, 36, 121

Celts, 92

census, 2, 33–41, 125
    1841 census, 37
    1881 census, 40–41, 122
    1911 census, 38–40

charity, 47

charts, 109–110

christening, 18

Church of England, 45

clan, 103, 105–106, 108, 128

clan badges, 106

cleared, 125

Clerk, 99
Cliff, 100
Clift, 8
coat of arms, 67
College of Arms, 69
Commonwealth War Graves
    Commission, 52
contacting relatives, 112, 134–
    136
Cooper, 100
Cornwall, 93, 104
costs, 145
counties, 80–81
Court of Lord Lyon, 68
cremation, 20
Curnow, 7, 104–105
Curthoys, 7
custom event, 133
Cyndi's List, 42–45, 129

daguerrotypes, 137
dame schools, 175
Danish Vikings, 93
dark ages, 3
Davis, 7, 99
death certificates, 21, 23, 85
death dates, 16
death records, 18–19, 21
deep DNA, 89, 91
dialect, 151–152
dialect dictionaries, 152

directories, 71–74
disease screening, 90
divorce, 20
DNA, 3, 15, 89–98
Doomsday Book, 33, 79
double–barrelled surname, 101
drawing family trees, 131
Dublin, 93
Durham, 100

electoral register, 135
Ellis Island, 157
emails, 135–136
emigration, 56
English Dialect Society, 152
Erridge, 105
estimates, 15–16
ethnic DNA, 89, 91
Everson, 7, 105

family Bible, 18, 19
family medical history, 84
family trees, 10, 15, 109
FamilyHistory.com, 121
FamilySearch.com, 125
Fanshaw, 101
Fetherstonehaugh, 101
finding relatives, 48, 134–136
first names, 106
first principles, 14
First World War, 50, 142

Fitz–Herbert, 101
FriendsReunited, 48, 123

Gaelic, 152
gateway ancestor, 66
GEDCOM, 124, 125, 127, 131–133
genealogist, 1
general labourer, 61
generation, 16
Generations Network, 120
GenesReunited, 48, 119, 123, 134
genetic heritage, 84
genetic tools, 10
Genghis Khan, 95
gentleman, 61
Germany, 121
Google, 12–13
graduation, 77
grammar school, 76
gravestones, 143
grazier, 61
Green, 100
Greenwich, 81
GRO, 49
Grosvenor, 100
Gypsy surnames, 101

hair, 149–150
Hall, 8

Harris, 101, 105
Harry Potter, 107
Hart, 101
heraldry, 69
Hertz, 101
history, 82
hobos, 64
hospital records, 85
hospitals, 41
hotel, 41
husbandman, 61

Iceland, 94
IGI, 27, 29–31
IGI batch numbers, 32
illegitimacy, 101
immigration, 56
inheritance, 101
innkeeper, 61
institutions, 41
Ireland, 23–24, 34, 93, 108
ISBN, 111
Isle of Man, 93

Jesus Christ Church of Latter
    Day Saints, 29, 120
jewellery, 148
Jewish first names, 106
Jewish surnames, 101
Johnson, 99
Jones, 7, 101, 104, 105

Jonsdottir, 99

Kent and Canterbury Press, 60
Kindred Connections, 125
kinship, 104–105

laird, 68–69
late–created surnames, 101
Lee, 105
Lemon, 101
libel, 133
life expectancy, 87
life peerage, 69
links list, 42–43
Liverpool, 81
local history, 15, 79–80, 111
local history societies, 80
local newspapers, 59
location surnames ,100
longevity, 87
look-up exchanges, 46–47
lord of the manor, 68

McAdam, 99
MacDonald, 99
Macleod, 95
maps, 80–81, 83
marriage, 16, 18–19, 21, 25–27
marriage certificates, 20, 22
marriage licence, 19
Martin, 8

matriculation, 77
Meadow, 100
medal card, 51
mediaeval records, 2
memorial inscriptions, 19, 21,
    76, 82
middle names, 17
migration, 56, 82
military records, 50–55, 82
miller, 61
mitochondrial DNA, 91, 94, 98
Moffat, 100
monogenesis, 7–8, 104
Morley, 105
Mormons, 29–30, 120, 125
mourning cards, 19
muscular dystrophy, 85
My Trees, 125

National Portrait Gallery, 144
National Trust Names, 4, 107
Native American, 92
newspapers, 18–19, 58–60, 146
New York, 57
New Zealand, 56
nicknames, 17, 100
nobility, 65–70
non–conformist, 46
Norton, 7, 68
Norwegian Vikings, 93, 94

obituaries, 146

occupational surnames, 99

occupations, 61–64

Oliver Twist, 63

O'Neill, 99

OneGreatFamily.com, 126

one-name studies, 89, 91, 128

oral history, 144

Palmer, 7, 100, 105, 149

parent search, 32

parish registers, 18–20, 27

passenger arrival lists, 57

paternity testing, 91

patronymics, 99

penny school, 75

photographs 14, 137–142

Plantagenet Roll of the Blood Royal, 67

polygenesis, 7, 8, 104

poor, 63–64, 82

Poor Law, 63

portraits, 142

posthumous baptism, 29, 125

Prince Harry, 107

prizes, 77

problems, 45, 131–133

public school, 76

Puritans, 106

Quakers, 106

Queen of England, 65, 67

Reardon, 101

recording family trees, 114–118

regimental histories, 52–53

regiments, 59

relatives, 10, 14–15, 17

remarriage, 101

Roman, 79

Roman Catholic, 106

Romany, 152

Rootsweb.com, 126

Roper, 101

Royal Stewart, 108

Rutland, 81

samplers, 148

scholar, 75

scholarships, 77

school, 75

Scotland, 93, 108, 152

search engine, 12

Second World War, 50, 52

sept, 101

settlements, 63

seven daughters of Eve, 91

Shakespeare, William, 103

shepherd, 61

ships, 59

shopkeeper, 61

single-name study, 48

Smith, 7, 99, 100, 104, 105
Smyth, 101
social class, 104
Soke of Peterborough, 81
Somme, battle of, 54
South Africa, 56
surname, 4–7, 67, 91, 94–95,
    99–108
surname profiling, 103–104
swagman, 64

tartan, 108
Tay Sachs disease, 85, 89
Taylor, 101
telephone directories, 71, 82
The Times, 58, 146
timeline, 83
titles, 67–69
trade directories, 71–74
traders, 73
trump cards, 124
twins, 86

university records, 75, 77–78
USA, 23–24, 36, 56, 121

Utah, 120, 125

Victoria, Queen, 2
video clips, 144
Vikings, 92, 94
village websites, 80
vital records, 22

Wales, 93
war memorial, 76
wedding groups, 142–143
Welsh, 152
White, 99, 105
Wickenden, 105
William the Conqueror, 100
wills, 55
work-arounds, 4
work-house, 41
working class, 82
World Family Tree, 124–125

Y-chromosome, 92, 94, 97–98
yeoman, 61
Yiddish, 152
Yorkshire, 81